Developing a Professional Teaching Portfolio

A Guide for Success

Patricia M. Costantino
Marie N. De Lorenzo

University of Maryland College Park

Allyn and Bacon

Boston • London • Toronto • Sydney • Tokyo • Singapore

Executive Editor and Publisher: Stephen D. Dragin
Series Editorial Assistant: Barbara Strickland
Marketing Manager: Amy Cronin
Production Editor: Annette Pagliaro
Editorial Production: Walsh & Associates, Inc.
Composition Buyer: Linda Cox
Manufacturing Buyer: Chris Marson
Cover Administrator: Kristina Mose-Libon
Electronic Composition: Publishers' Design and Production Services, Inc.

Copyright © 2002 by Allyn & Bacon
A Pearson Education Company
75 Arlington Street
Boston, MA 02116

Internet: www.ablongman.com

All rights reserved. No part of the material protected by this copyright notice
may be reproduced or utilized in any form or by any means, electronic or
mechanical, including photocopying, recording, or by any information storage
and retrieval system, without written permission from the copyright owner.

Library of Congress Cataloging-in-Publication Data

Costantino, Patricia M.
    Developing a professional teaching portfolio : a guide for success /
Patricia M. Costantino, Marie N. De Lorenzo.
        p.   cm
    Includes bibliographical references (p.) and index.
    ISBN 0-205-32955-1
    1. Teachers—Rating of—United States.   2. Teachers—Training of—United
States.   3. Portfolios in education—United States.   I. De Lorenzo, Marie N.
II. Title.
LB1728 .C67 2002
371.14'4—dc21

                                                                                2001046341

Printed in the United States of America
10 9 8 7 6 5   05 04

Contents

Preface   vii

Chapter 1: Understanding the Concept   1

What Is a Professional Teaching Portfolio?   2

Types of Portfolios   2
  Preservice Teacher Portfolios   3
  Inservice Teacher Portfolios   4

Benefits of Portfolio Development   4
  Fostering Self-Assessment and Reflection   4
  Providing Personal Satisfaction and Renewal   5
  Providing Tools for Empowerment   5
  Promoting Collaboration   5
  Providing Holistic Approach to Assessment   6

Portfolio Development Issues   6
  Labor-Intensive and Time-Consuming Preparation   6
  Presentation of Documents   6
  Evaluation of Portfolio Documents   7

Reviewing Chapter 1   8

Chapter 2: Portfolio Development and Performance Standards   9

Background   9

Linking Performance Standards to Teaching and
    Portfolio Development   10
  Teaching Standards Correlated with Student Standards   10
  Targeted Outcomes   10
  Credibility   10
  Common Language   11
  *Current Trends in Teaching Assessment and Evaluation
      Complemented   11*
  Performance Standards and Coursework   12
  Performance Standards and a Professional Development Plan   13

Reviewing Chapter 2   21

Chapter 3: Phase I—Getting Started   23

Determining the Purpose   23

Considering a Set of Performance Standards   23

Collecting, Selecting, and Creating Documents   24
  Suggestions for Portfolio Documentation   24

Reviewing Chapter 3   28

Chapter 4:   Phase II—Enhancing Your Documents   29

Connecting Standards to Portfolio Documentation   29

Supporting Your Documents   30
  Introductions   31
  Explanations   31
  Reflections   31

Displaying Your Documents   32
  Housing   33
  Organizing   35
  Formatting   35

Turning a Teaching Experience into a Portfolio Entry   36

Reviewing Chapter 4   39

Chapter 5:   Phase III—Using Your Portfolio   41

Self-Evaluating Your Portfolio   41
  Evaluating the Introduction and Organization of Your Portfolio   42
  Evaluating Your Use of Performance Standards,
    Themes, or Goals   42
  Evaluating Your Documentation   42
  Evaluating Your Introductions, Explanations, and Reflections   43

Presenting Your Portfolio   44

Reviewing Chapter 5   46

Chapter 6:   Electronic Portfolios: An Option   47

What Is an Electronic Portfolio?   47

Why Should I Consider Developing an Electronic Portfolio?   48

Do I Have the Technological Knowledge and Skills?   49

What Computer Hardware Will I Need?   49

What Computer Software Will I Need?   50

Options and Issues When Publishing an Electronic Portfolio   51
  Publishing on a CD-ROM   51
  Publishing on the Internet   51

Where Can I Get Additional Information and
  See Actual Examples?   52

Helpful Hints   53
Reviewing Chapter 6   55

Chapter 7:   Examples of Portfolio Entries   57
About This Chapter   57
Examples of Introductory Artifacts   58
Examples of Instructional Artifacts   71

Appendices

A: **Examples of Standards   99**

B: **Professional Organizations   107**

C: **Worksheet: Linking Coursework and Standards to Portfolio Documents   111**

D: **Sample Permission Letter for Photographs and/or Videotapes   113**

E: **Including a Videotape in Your Portfolio   115**

F: **Worksheet: Making Decisions About Potential Portfolio Documents   117**

G: **Worksheet: Self-Evaluation   123**

H: **Overall Portfolio Assessment Instrument   127**

I: **Example Portfolio Contents   131**

Glossary   141

References   145

Index   149

Preface

This handbook is intended to be a practical resource for successfully developing a professional teaching portfolio. It breaks down the process of portfolio development into a step-by-step approach to reduce the stress of engaging in this rigorous endeavor. It is also practical in that it discusses how performance standards provide a solid foundation for the selection of artifacts. Finally, it is practical in that the many examples of portfolio entries from teacher candidates and experienced teachers provide a variety of ideas from those who have traveled this same journey.

We believe that teacher candidates, experienced teachers, college professors, supervisors, staff developers, and administrators will find this handbook a valuable resource of information and ideas for use in preservice and inservice programs that require or recommend professional teaching portfolios. We are also convinced that the process and product of portfolio development is one of the most beneficial activities that an individual can pursue for his or her own professional development.

The following teachers and teacher candidates have graciously allowed us to include their portfolio materials in this handbook: Rosanna Calabrese, Emily Anne Cosden, Lauren T. Costas, Matt DeMunbrun, Carol Dungan, Merritt Imbriale, Ryan Imbriale, Denise Logsdon, Kate Maczis, Jeff Maher, Maria Giovanna Marsili, Scott Mooney, and Lisa Wehausen. We are deeply indebted to them. In addition, we would like to thank Dr. Deborah Kraft, Villa Julie College, and Dr. Rebecca K. Fox, George Mason University for allowing us to include their portfolio evaluation instruments. We would also like to recognize our colleagues in the College of Education at the University of Maryland for their assistance and support. In particular, we would like to thank Dr. William De Lorenzo and Dr. Christy Corbin for the numerous hours they contributed to reviewing our manuscript. We would also like to thank the following reviewers for their time and input: Carol Pelletier, Boston College; Judy R. Wilkerson, University of Southern Florida; and Judy A. Werner, Slippery Rock University.

Creating a professional portfolio is a challenging and rigorous endeavor. It can also be one of the most meaningful and rewarding experiences in a teacher's professional development. We hope that you will find this handbook to be a valuable professional resource.

1 Understanding the Concept

THE USE OF A PROFESSIONAL TEACHING PORTFOLIO has become increasingly valued in the field of education. School systems and teacher education institutions are now considering portfolio development as a worthwhile process for documenting teaching performance, fostering professional growth, and facilitating reflective thinking. A teacher's portfolio is one of the many approaches that may be considered to determine the effectiveness of a teacher. When a portfolio is used in conjunction with other forms of assessment, it can provide a broader perspective of a teacher's full range of professional competencies.

In light of the increased interest in portfolios, we have developed this handbook to help you understand the concept of a professional teaching portfolio and to assist you in the process of portfolio development. This set of practical guidelines includes information and materials to help prospective and practicing teachers communicate their teaching effectiveness and professional accomplishments through a portfolio. It provides information for creating a meaningful and useful portfolio relevant to your purpose. These guidelines may be adapted to many types of educational personnel; however, the focus of this handbook is primarily on the use of portfolios for:

Preservice Teacher Candidates Who
- Are required to a develop a portfolio to document their professional growth and learning.
- Are seeking initial employment and choose to use a portfolio to enhance the job search and interview process.

Inservice Teachers Who
- Are documenting their teaching performance as a component of the teacher evaluation process.
- Are fulfilling recertification or continuing professional development requirements.
- Are seeking career advancement, making lateral moves within the school system, or relocating and choose to use a portfolio to enhance this process.

The information, worksheets, and examples in this handbook are designed to increase your understanding of:

- The concept of a professional teaching portfolio
- The value of considering performance standards when documenting teaching competencies and accomplishments
- The phases of portfolio development
- Electronic portfolios
- The variety of artifacts that can be included in a portfolio

What Is a Professional Teaching Portfolio?

The current teacher education literature is replete with definitions of the professional teaching portfolio. Bird (1990) defines portfolios as an organized set of documents that provide evidence of a teacher's knowledge, dispositions, and skills in the complex art of teaching. Brown and Wolfe-Quintero (1997) state that portfolios are a "purposeful collection of any aspect of a teacher's work that tells the story of the teacher's efforts, skills, abilities, achievement, and contributions to his or her students, colleagues, institution, academic discipline or community" (p. 28). Evans (1995) concludes that "A professional portfolio is an evolving collection of carefully selected or composed professional thoughts, goals and experiences that are threaded with reflection and self-assessment. It represents who you are, what you do, why you do it, where you have been, where you are, where you want to go, and how you plan on getting there" (p. 11). In general, the definitions share many common elements. They consistently affirm the idea that portfolio documentation provides authentic evidence of a teacher's work and is a vehicle for fostering reflection on the art and practice of teaching.

Types of Portfolios

Many kinds of portfolios are developed by teacher education candidates and school system teachers. The types of portfolios described in this handbook parallel the definitions of portfolios discussed throughout the literature. Although different terms may be used, the intent is similar. The following information will clarify several types of portfolios that are typically used by preservice and inservice teachers.*

---

* For the purpose of this handbook, the terms "preservice teacher candidate" and "inservice teacher" will be referred to as "teacher," except in cases where the specific term is more appropriate. The terms "portfolio documents," "documentation," "artifacts," "entries," and "materials" are used interchangeably when referring to the contents of a portfolio.

Preservice Teacher Portfolios

Many performance-based teacher education programs are moving toward the use of portfolios to admit, monitor, and evaluate teacher candidates (Barry & Shannon, 1997; Guillaume & Yopp, 1995; Rakow, 1999). The ongoing nature of the portfolio development process provides the opportunity for teacher candidates, college faculty, cooperating teachers, and field supervisors to dialogue and reflect on a teacher candidate's growth and learning throughout the entire program. Four types of *preservice* teacher portfolios are described below.

Entrance Portfolio—This type of portfolio may be required by teacher education programs as a component of the admission screening process. The materials in this portfolio are intended to provide information about an individual's prior knowledge, skills, dispositions, and experiences that support his or her potential to be successful in a teacher education program.

(Process Portfolio)

Working Portfolio—A working portfolio is a vehicle for documenting growth and development toward performance standards and teacher education program requirements. The intent of this type of portfolio is to integrate academic coursework and field experiences so that there is a meaningful connection between theory, practice, and the artifacts presented in the portfolio. The literature often refers to this type of portfolio as a *process portfolio* (Antonek, McCormic, & Donato, 1997). The materials included in this portfolio provide evidence of a teacher candidate's accomplishments at various benchmarks throughout the program. They reflect *work in progress* and growth over time and are not intended to be polished documents. The teacher candidate meets with college faculty, field supervisors, and cooperating teachers using portfolio documents as a basis for discussing teaching performance and areas for continued growth.

Exit Portfolio—Exit portfolios are a final selection of artifacts that provide substantial evidence of a teacher candidate's level of mastery related to performance standards and the goals of the program. These portfolios are usually evaluated by individuals affiliated with the teacher education program and are rated using scoring rubrics. Many colleges of education require teacher candidates to formally present their portfolios as a part of the requirements for successful completion of their teacher education program.

Interview Portfolio—The artifacts in this portfolio are a subset of the best work from the working and exit portfolio. Antonek and colleagues (1997) refer to this type of portfolio as a *product portfolio*. The intent of this type of portfolio is to limit the number of artifacts to create a showcase of exemplary documents representative of a teacher candidate's *best work* and accomplishments for the purpose of gaining employment.

Inservice Teacher Portfolios

While some school districts are not yet requiring that teachers develop professional portfolios, many are using portfolios to support national and state initiatives toward performance-based assessment and continued professional development for inservice teachers. In addition, portfolios are being developed by teachers to support their career enhancement efforts. The working and showcase portfolio are typical of inservice teacher portfolios.

Working Portfolio—A working portfolio for the inservice teacher is similar to that of a teacher candidate. The major difference is that the inservice teacher works collaboratively with the school administration to identify goals for continued professional growth related to the total school improvement plan. The portfolio becomes a vehicle for documenting accomplishment toward those goals. A working portfolio may be utilized in conjunction with the ongoing teacher observation/evaluation process and established performance standards of the school or school system.

Showcase Portfolio—This portfolio parallels the teacher candidate interview portfolio. It is a *polished* collection of exemplary documents that highlight a teacher's best work and accomplishments. Teachers may use this type of portfolio for informally sharing information about themselves with colleagues, administrators, parents, and community members. It may also be used for more goal-motivated purposes such as obtaining leadership roles, seeking job advancement, making lateral moves, fulfilling requirements for recertification, or making a career change.

Benefits of Portfolio Development

There are many benefits to portfolio development. These benefits range from personal to professional.

Fostering Self-Assessment and Reflection

Barton and Collins (1993) claim that portfolios foster the development of self-assessment and reflective thinking. The process of portfolio development requires a teacher to identify episodes of teaching, analyze what occurred, and assess the effectiveness of his or her teaching performance and the outcomes of student learning. Teachers become researchers of their own practice (Bartel, Kaye, & Morin, 1998). Wolfe and Dietz (1998) indicate that depending on the purpose, portfolios have the potential to "stimulate and strengthen teacher reflection and practice" and "provide a comprehensive and authentic evaluation of a teacher's performance" (p. 6).

Providing Personal Satisfaction and Renewal

In 1995, a task force of the National School Reform Faculty (NSRF) implemented a project that required teachers to examine and reflect on their own work by using the portfolio format (Cushman, 1999). The results of this project provided testimonials from inservice teachers which further confirmed the benefits of portfolio development. Most of the educators who participated in this project stated that "developing their portfolios gave them a sense of personal satisfaction, sometimes, even exhilaration, from what they had learned" (p. 749). One participant stated: "It forces me to constantly and consistently look at what I'm doing, making sure that what I'm doing is good — for students and for me—and to improve. You can't stay stagnant" (p. 749). A veteran of thirty years of teaching was eager to use the portfolio process as a source of new insights. He claimed that developing a portfolio "breathed new life into his practice" (p. 749).

Providing Tools for Empowerment

Portfolios can be tools for empowerment. They encourage teachers to assume more responsibility and ownership for their own learning and professional growth. Inservice teachers can become self-directed to identify their goals and plans for continued professional growth instead of depending on an administrator to determine their teaching effectiveness through one or two yearly evaluations.

Anderson and DeMeulle (1998) found that preservice teachers who use portfolios are "more knowledgeable about issues related to the complexity of teaching, self-assessment, and about understanding that learning is an ongoing process" (p. 24). They also found that teacher candidates are confident enough to reflect on their own learning. Learning to teach is not only determined by the number of courses taken, but through multiple experiences; coursework, clinical field experiences, research, seminars, and other educational activities that contribute to their professional growth. Teacher candidates become responsible for integrating and documenting the knowledge, dispositions, and skills they learned through these experiences in their professional portfolio. The process of reflecting and documenting what they know and are able to do is highly empowering and contributes to their self confidence as novice teachers.

Promoting Collaboration

Using the portfolio process as a method of evaluating teaching performance provides the opportunity for a teacher to engage in a collaborative discussion with the reviewer and to receive formative feedback and guidance on a regular basis. This collaborative event is highly personalized with the intent to promote self-reflection and the improvement of teaching skills. It can lead to a mutual identification of goals for ongoing professional growth.

Providing Holistic Approach to Assessment

Portfolios provide multiple sources of evidence that are not apparent in traditional assessments. Therefore, a portfolio is a more authentic tool for evaluating teacher growth and learning (Barton & Collins, 1993). Many individuals do not perform well on standardized tests. Items included in a portfolio, such as original lesson plans, evidence of student learning, written feedback from observations and evaluations, and reflective journal entries, present a holistic view of one's achievement as opposed to a resume, transcripts, or test results. Portfolios are an important assessment option because they add the breath and depth that may not be present in more traditional evaluation methods (Hunter, 1998).

Portfolio Development Issues

It is not enough to cite the benefits of portfolio development without recognizing that there are dilemmas inherent in this process.

Labor-Intensive and Time-Consuming Preparation

One of most often mentioned issues is that the process of portfolio development is labor intensive and time consuming (Wheeler, 1993). Many preservice teachers feel overwhelmed at the thought of having to develop a portfolio (Stone, 1998). A remedy to this dilemma is for teacher candidates to start collecting potential documents early in their teacher education program. In addition, a reflective journal will help the teacher candidate to remember how these documents contributed to his or her professional growth and learning. The earlier time is invested in the collection and reflection process, the easier it will be to prepare an *exit* or *interview* portfolio. This will help eliminate the stress associated with beginning the process during student teaching.

Inservice teachers may feel that they need to document everything they have accomplished. This is an unreasonable self-imposed expectation. Identification of a realistic set of professional goals with a small number of artifacts that best support these goals will make the task more manageable.

Presentation of Documents

Another issue is the reality that some teachers know how to package materials and market themselves better than others (Wheeler, 1993).

Teachers who are very artistic or have access to superior technological resources are able to easily assemble a visually pleasing and impressive product. This places the teacher without that talent or resources at a disadvantage and may affect the scoring process when the portfolio is used for interview or evaluation purposes. The key is to make sure that the substance of the documents and reflective entries are exemplary. First impressions are critical, therefore, a neat and well-organized portfolio is essential.

Evaluation of Portfolio Documents

Another major concern is the identification of an acceptable method of assessing portfolios. The selection of portfolio products is usually left to the discretion of the portfolio developer. This is a highly individualized process and unique to each person. While this is one of the most beneficial aspects for the use of portfolios, it presents a problem when portfolios are used in the evaluation process. The more diverse the documentation, the more difficult it becomes to compare and evaluate the portfolio. Evaluation is dependent on the professional judgment of the reviewer and is highly subjective. An often selected solution to this problem is the use of a rubric or Likert-type evaluation scale, which includes the aspects of performance to be measured and the criteria for rating those aspects. It is in the best interest of teachers to become familiar with the instruments used to rate portfolio documentation by their teacher education program or school system. Becoming familiar with the specific rating criteria will help the teacher to select appropriate documentation which meets the standards determined by their program or school system. Examples of portfolio scoring rubrics can be found in Appendix I.

It is obvious that there are many issues associated with portfolio development. Despite this, the literature shows that the benefits of portfolio development outweigh the drawbacks. Portfolios are one of the most authentic ways to represent the knowledge, dispositions, and skills of a teacher. As stated earlier, when used with other methods of evaluating teacher performance, portfolios can provide a broader perspective of a teacher's full range of professional competencies.

Reviewing Chapter 1

The information presented in this chapter was intended to provide you with an understanding of the concept of a professional teaching portfolio. Use these questions as a review for yourself and as an opportunity to meaningfully link the information to your individual situation or portfolio purpose.

How would the development of professional teaching portfolio benefit you?

_____

_____

At this time, what type of portfolio best suits your purpose?

_____

_____

Which portfolio development issue is most troublesome to you and how will you deal with it?

_____

_____

Now that you have a basic understanding of the concept of a professional portfolio, the types of portfolios, and the benefits and issues related to portfolio development, you are ready to learn about the relationship between performance standards and portfolio development.

2 Portfolio Development and Performance Standards

Background

The national focus on performance standards for teachers is grounded in the proposition that high standards for student achievement can best be reached if teachers have the knowledge and skills necessary to prepare students to meet these standards. In 1987 the National Board for Professional Teaching Standards (NBPTS) was created to establish high and rigorous standards for what accomplished teachers should know and be able to do. In the same year, the Interstate New Teacher Assessment and Support Consortium (INTASC) was established to restructure teacher assessment for initial licensing as well as for preparation and induction into the profession. INTASC developed performance standards for what beginning teachers should know and be able to do. The NBPTS and INTASC agree that the complex art of teaching requires performance based standards.

In 1997, the National Commission on Teaching and America's Future published a report that challenged the nation and its teacher preparation institutions to become serious about performance standards for teachers. Responding to the National Commission's recommendation regarding standards, many versions of teaching performance standards have been developed by national groups and associations, colleges of education, state departments of education, and local education agencies for the purpose of teacher preparation, initial licensing, and continuing professional development. The national standards for beginning and experienced teachers have provided the foundation for a unifying vision that is needed to ensure consistency and compatibility with the many approaches to teacher preparation and professional development. The development and use of performance standards is seen as a way to facilitate the professionalization of teaching and to shape the practice of those who prepare teachers (Bartell, 1998). Bernauer (1999) states: "Standards offer a way to develop criteria for assessing growth and effectiveness of instructional practices. Standards can help identify clear targets for student outcomes" (p. 68). The ultimate intent of standards is to improve the quality of teaching and increase student achievement.

All performance standards, whether national, state, or local, are based upon shared views within the educational community of what constitutes professional teaching. Each set of standards captures the knowledge, dispositions, and skills related to effective teaching. Linda

Darling-Hammond (Darling-Hammond, Wise, & Klein, 1995) defines these attributes as follows: *Professional knowledge* includes a grounding in the many areas that provide an understanding of students and their learning (p. 38); *teaching dispositions* are the orientations teachers develop to think and behave in professionally responsive ways (p. 39); *teaching skills* include the abilities to transform knowledge into actions needed for effective teaching (p. 39). It is evident that the standards movement has significantly influenced all aspects of the teaching profession from teacher training, to initial licensure, to national certification. Standards identify the heart and core of what it takes to be an effective teacher.

Linking Performance Standards to Teaching and Portfolio Development

Having a basic understanding of performance standards is important. Just as critical is the understanding of how these standards are meaningfully linked to the practice of teaching and portfolio development. The following information provides a rationale supporting the importance of performance standards and their relationship to teaching and professional portfolios.

Teaching Standards Correlated with Student Standards

Performance standards for teachers are directly correlated to performance standards for student learning (Ambach, 1996). What teachers know and are able to do is the most important influence on what students learn (National Commission on Teaching, 1997). Teachers need to demonstrate their own competency in order to validate their ability to promote student achievement.

Targeted Outcomes

Standards provide teachers with targeted outcomes in the knowledge, dispositions, and skills related to effective teaching. Targeted outcomes allow teacher candidates to monitor their own growth toward program requirements and help experienced teachers to identify goals for professional growth based on accepted standards of the profession.

Credibility

Using national or state standards when developing a portfolio provides credibility to the documentation. Portfolio artifacts should be selected or created to directly support and validate a teacher's competency toward a performance standard as opposed to the arbitrary selection and display of materials. Furthermore, INTASC standards for beginning teachers are currently being used across the nation for initial certification of teachers. Performance criteria, not coursework, will become the new standard for licensure (Draper, 1998). Teacher candidates will be responsible for collecting appropriate documentation for initial certification related to performance standards. In addition, the NBPTS for accomplished teachers requires the use of standards in portfolio development for national certification. Inservice teachers who consider performance standards when developing their portfolio will be in step with the current national and state reform initiatives for high standards for teaching performance.

Common Language

Using standards provides a common language that is understood by most portfolio reviewers. Regardless of which set of standards is considered, there is a common core of teaching knowledge, dispositions, and skills that have similar outcomes but are stated differently. Therefore, a portfolio utilizing standards can be appropriate and acceptable in many situations. This can be especially beneficial when applying for employment or licensure in different geographical areas.

Current Trends in Teaching Assessment and Evaluation Complemented

Many performance-based teacher education programs are designed around national or state standards. Performance assessment instruments are being developed by colleges of education to assess teacher candidate competency in meeting the standards. In addition, school systems are using performance standards to evaluate teacher growth and ongoing professional development. Therefore, considering standards when developing a portfolio will provide a natural alignment with standards-based assessment and evaluation.

Several examples of national standards can be found in Appendix A of this handbook. They are *representative* of the many sets of standards established by national, state, and local organizations. These examples provide an overview of the standards and do not include the full range of knowledge, dispositions, and skills inherent in the complete set. The overviews presented are the INTASC standards for beginning teachers and NBPTS standards for accomplished teachers. Also included is an example of standards developed by the Council for Exceptional Children (CEC). Other sets of standards may be selected to meet individual content or specialty areas. Appendix B includes a list of professional organizations that have developed content or specialty area performance standards.

As indicated earlier, standards are shared views within the educational community of what constitutes professional teaching. Although the standards may be stated differently by various national, state, or local agencies or organizations, the performance outcomes are similar. In fact, when comparing the standards of various organizations, several themes emerge:

- Knowledge of subject matter
- Planning, delivery, and assessment of instruction
- Classroom management and organization
- Human relationships
- Professionalism

It is not uncommon for teachers to consider using these or other themes to guide the selection of documents for their portfolio. Both standards and themes provide a credible theoretical foundation for a portfolio. This handbook uses the terms *standards* and *themes* interchangeably when discussing the relationship of portfolio artifacts to performance standards.

The remainder of this chapter is devoted to explaining how teacher candidates can link performance standards to coursework and field experiences and how both inservice teachers and teacher candidates can use performance standards in correlation with their professional development plan.

Performance Standards and Coursework

Performance standards for teacher candidates are identified by their specific teacher education program. These standards range from the INTASC standards for beginning teachers to specific content area standards developed by professional organizations to state-mandated standards for licensure. Knowing the expected performance standards of their teacher education program enables teacher candidates to make connections between required coursework and field experiences.

Each course that is taken should meaningfully relate to one or more of the performance standards. The assignments, readings, research papers, and special projects identified in the course syllabus should all contribute to the acquisition of the knowledge, dispositions, and skills described in the standards. Similarly, field experiences will also need to be meaningfully linked to performance standards. Therefore, a teacher candidate will need to give considerable thought to how ongoing teaching responsibilities (such as designing lessons, delivering instruction, assessing student learning, managing the classroom, attending professional activities, communicating with colleagues, and working with diversity) fit into supporting his or her growth toward a performance standard. The more familiar one becomes with the standards, the easier it will be to see the connections between coursework, clinical field experiences, and the standards. By routinely analyzing how coursework and field experiences contribute to meeting the performance standards, teacher candidates can become highly reflective while creating an ongoing record of their growth and development throughout their entire program.

Figure 2.1, on page 14, illustrates how a teacher candidate might systematically envision the connection between coursework, clinical field experiences, and growth toward a performance standard. This type of chart can be used throughout the entire teacher education program. The teacher candidate begins by identifying the course and assignments that significantly contribute to his or her knowledge, dispositions, and skills related to the standard. He or she then reflects on what occurred, what was learned, and what portfolio documents should be included in the portfolio.

Performance Standards and a Professional Development Plan

A professional development plan delineates a teacher's goals for short- and/or long-term professional growth. These goals should be aligned with the performance standards identified by the school system or teacher preparation program. The inservice teacher's professional development plan is focused on continued professional growth related to performance evaluations and/or individual career objectives. The teacher candidate's professional development plan is related to coursework, field experiences, and the required performance outcomes of the teacher education program.

Figure 2.2, on pages 15–17, describes a process for creating a professional development plan related to performance standards and the practice of teaching. The intent of this process is to facilitate reflection and to improve teaching effectiveness. This chart is an example of a professional development plan that focuses on a goal related to cooperative learning strategies.

This seven-step approach can be invaluable at the inservice and preservice levels. It requires collaborative planning, focused dialogue, and ongoing communication between the teacher and those individuals who guide and support the development of professional portfolios. It can provide the structure for conversations between a teacher and an administrator or a university faculty member during an evaluation conference. It can be the tool for empowering the teacher to identify his or her professional goals, or it could provide the structure for collaborative decision making that sets the direction for a teacher's ongoing professional development. In this approach, teaching becomes a collaborative event with discussion based on the identification of teaching goals and the design of purposeful plans for continued professional development.

Directions:
- Identify the course.
- List the assignments.
- Determine how the assignment contributed to your knowledge, disposition, and skills.
- Identify the appropriate performance standard or theme.
- Reflect in writing what you learned.
- Consider what could be placed in your portfolio to capture this experience.

Course	Assignment	Knowledge	Dispositions	Skills	Standard(s)
Human Development and Learning	Case Study -3rd grade child	Vygotsky's Theory of Sociocultural Development -Scaffolding	I believe that learning occurs when children are supported in their efforts to increase knowledge. Scaffolding requires teachers to provide appropriate materials, guidance, and questioning to bring the individual learner to a higher or new level (example science—exploration of primary and secondary colors provides a wealth of learning opportunities when a child is prompted toward discovery through opportunity and questioning).	- Observation of student behavior. - Assessment of prior knowledge on the part of individual learners. - Individualizing instruction.	INTASC Standards 4, 7, 8 Planning, delivery, and assessment of instruction

Reflection: *Observation of case study subject helped me realize the effectiveness of teacher scaffolding on the learning process. Children are more likely to attain new knowledge when they are questioned and supported while exploring new concepts/mediums.*

Possible Portfolio Documents: *Written observation of child being scaffolded by the teacher.*

Course	Assignment	Knowledge	Dispositions	Skills	Standard(s)
Assessment, Instruction, and Curriculum for Students with Severe Disabilities	*To write a functional domestic living program on a student's morning grooming routine*	*Life skills instruction relevant to independent community; personal living, and employment*	*Special educators should provide learning opportunities in a variety of environments including the home, the school, and the community*	*Select, adapt, and use instruction strategies and materials according to characteristics of the learner*	*CEC Common Core: K6; S8 Planning and delivery of instruction*

Reflection: *This domestic living program was based on documented patterns of behavior and data from informal assessment tools. Insight was gained into the importance of assessing skills prior to designing supports and adaptations. I realized the need to solicit feedback from the parents and siblings of the student to facilitate instructional delivery.*

Possible Portfolio Documents: *Interview format and results with parents and siblings; task analysis of morning grooming routine.*

See Appendix C for a blank chart for your personal use.

FIGURE 2.1 Linking coursework to standards and portfolio documents.

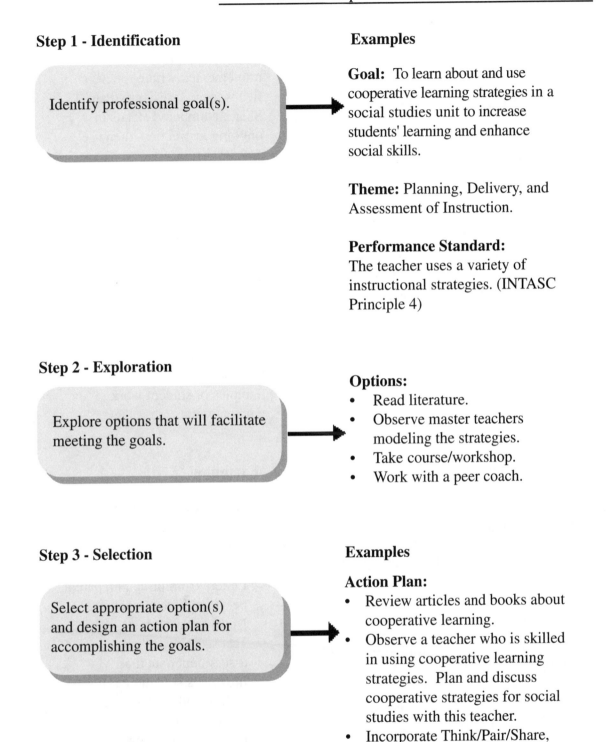

Step 1 - Identification

Identify professional goal(s).

Examples

Goal: To learn about and use cooperative learning strategies in a social studies unit to increase students' learning and enhance social skills.

Theme: Planning, Delivery, and Assessment of Instruction.

Performance Standard: The teacher uses a variety of instructional strategies. (INTASC Principle 4)

Step 2 - Exploration

Explore options that will facilitate meeting the goals.

Options:
- Read literature.
- Observe master teachers modeling the strategies.
- Take course/workshop.
- Work with a peer coach.

Step 3 - Selection

Select appropriate option(s) and design an action plan for accomplishing the goals.

Examples

Action Plan:
- Review articles and books about cooperative learning.
- Observe a teacher who is skilled in using cooperative learning strategies. Plan and discuss cooperative strategies for social studies with this teacher.
- Incorporate Think/Pair/Share, Numbered Heads, and Jigsaw in social studies lessons.

(continues)

FIGURE 2.2   Process for creating a professional development plan related to performance standards and the practice of teaching.

Step 4 - Implementation

Implement the plan.

The above plan will be implemented within the next five weeks. Use Think/Pair/Share, Numbered Heads in ongoing instruction, then use Jigsaw to reinforce student learning.

Step 5 - Documentation

Select and/or develop documents that illustrate implementation of the plan. *(Display as a portfolio entry with an introduction or explanation.)*

- Lesson plans and worksheets.
- A list and explanation of all cooperative learning strategies explored.
- Photographs/videotape of lesson(s) using cooperative learning with accompanying explanations.
- Samples of student work with captions.

Step 6 - Validation

Collect documents that verify teaching competency and accomplishments as well as results of instruction and student learning.

Examples

- Observation feedback and written evaluation from colleagues, administrators and supervisors.
- Letters from principal, parent, peers, and other teachers.
- Notes from students.
- Test scores or other assessment data that illustrates student learning.
- Before and after samples of student work.
- Explanation of how cooperative learning strategies increased student learning and improved social skills.

(continues)

FIGURE 2.2   (Continued).

Step 7 - Reflection

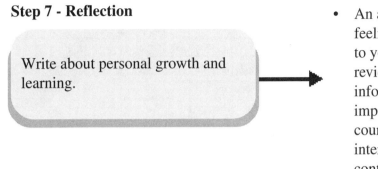

Write about personal growth and learning.

- An analysis of thoughts, feelings, and learnings related to your goal that provides the reviewer with more information to understand the impact of an activity, project, course, experience, or intervention, and how it contributed to your professional growth and student learning.

FIGURE 2.2   (Continued).

The following examples show how a teacher can represent his or her professional development plan as a portfolio document.

Figure 2.3, on page 18, illustrates how the seven-step approach could be represented in a portfolio. This professional development plan template consolidates the evidence of how a goal was accomplished by highlighting the essentials of a social studies unit that incorporates cooperative learning strategies. In reality, this type of entry may require more than one page to fully capture the richness of this unit of instruction.

Figure 2.4, on page 19, illustrates how a teacher planned for the inclusion of specific documents that support a standard related to her professional goal.

The portfolio entries shown in Figure 2.5, on page 20, communicate a professional development plan with goals related to technology and classroom management standards. The *Essential Dimensions of Teaching* are state standards selected by this college as a framework for portfolio documentation.

It is evident that standards are a driving force in educational reform. Teachers are now being held accountable for higher levels of performance based on national and or state standards. They can no longer merely submit a transcript or proclaim that they have the knowledge, dispositions, and skills required of an effective teacher. They must present authentic evidence of what they know, what they are able to do, and how their teaching increases student achievement. Serious consideration of performance standards when developing a professional portfolio will help teachers create and collect meaningful and focused portfolio documentation.

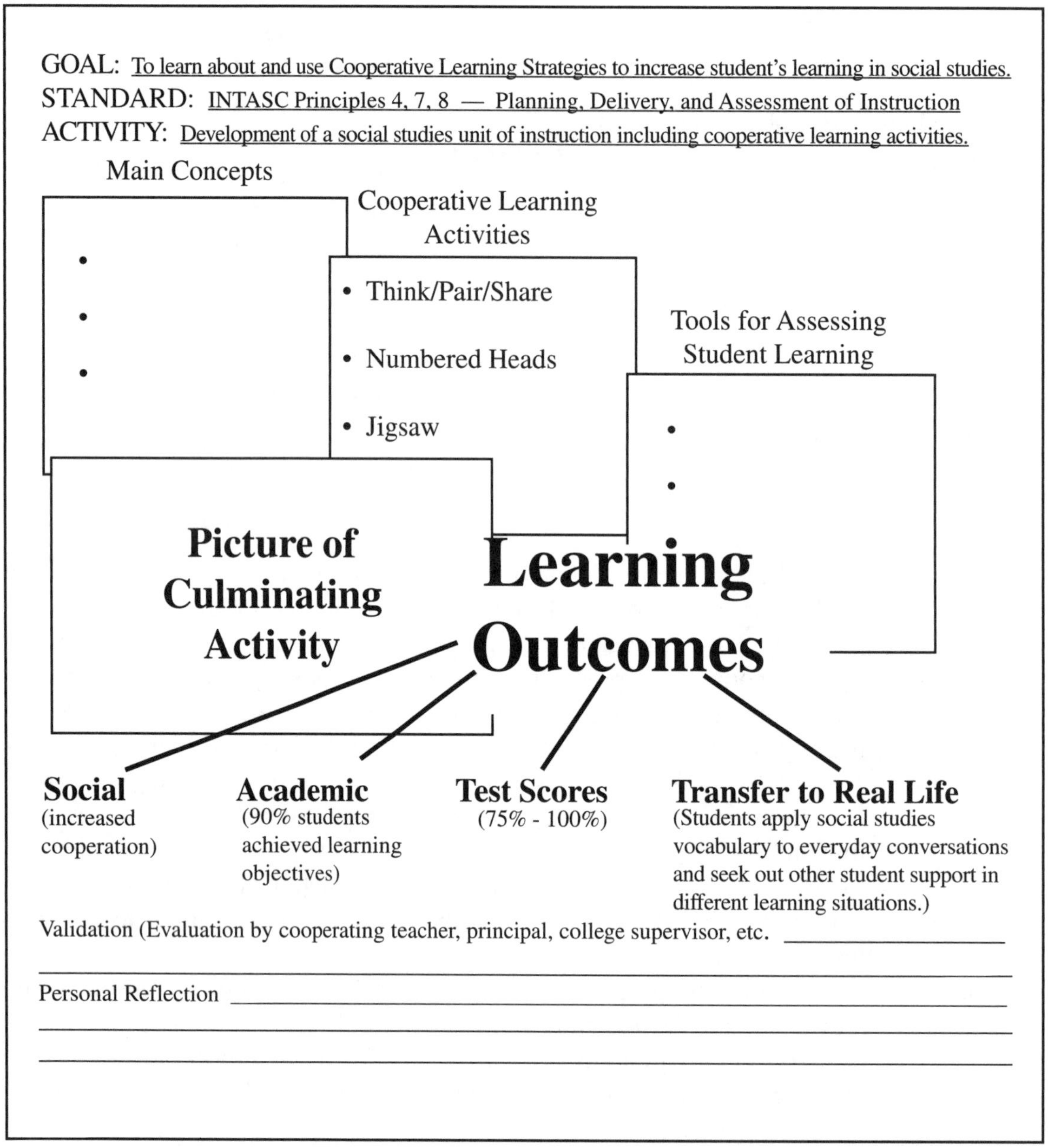

GOAL: To learn about and use Cooperative Learning Strategies to increase student's learning in social studies.
STANDARD: INTASC Principles 4, 7, 8 — Planning, Delivery, and Assessment of Instruction
ACTIVITY: Development of a social studies unit of instruction including cooperative learning activities.

Main Concepts

-
-
-

Cooperative Learning
Activities

- Think/Pair/Share

- Numbered Heads

- Jigsaw

Tools for Assessing
Student Learning

-
-

Picture of Culminating Activity

Learning Outcomes

Social
(increased cooperation)

Academic
(90% students achieved learning objectives)

Test Scores
(75% - 100%)

Transfer to Real Life
(Students apply social studies vocabulary to everyday conversations and seek out other student support in different learning situations.)

Validation (Evaluation by cooperating teacher, principal, college supervisor, etc. _____

Personal Reflection _____

FIGURE 2.3   Representing the seven-step approach as a portfolio entry.

Goal/Standard	Activities/Portfolio Documentation	How Do Your Documents Support Growth toward the Goal or Standard?
Goal: To make children and their families feel valued and important in the educational partnership. Standards: NBPTS—Family Partnerships NAEYC—Establishing reciprocal relationships with families	• Monthly newsletters (from teacher to families) • Photographs — of cubbies, which include photos of family members — of family/school events — of the Parent Bulletin Board posted outside of the classroom — of parents teaching/ sharing a skill with the children • Samples of resources shared with families (e.g., pamphlets, brochures, articles, etc.) • An invitation to parents requesting their attendance at a special event (e.g., picnic, holiday celebration, sing-along, etc.) • A cassette tape from the listening center, which has a parent reading a story or playing music. • A handout that summarizes what children gain from interactions within each of the learning centers (e.g., blocks, art, dramatic play, sand/water play, etc.)	Documents provide evidence the child is valued as a member of a family unit and family is integral to the functioning of the school as well as the curriculum. Moreover, family members are viewed as important contributors to the learning environment.

Courtesy of Christy Corbin

FIGURE 2.4   Professional goals chart.

Goal I:
To discover ways in which technology can be used appropriately and effectively in the classroom

Essential Dimensions of Teaching: Standard 1

Action Plan:
1) Evaluate several software programs
2) Review and cite at least three pieces of educational literature related to technology use in the classroom
3) Construct lessons that integrate technology

Professional Development Plan

Documentation:
1) Create a chart exhibiting summaries and uses for personally preferred software programs
2) Make an annotated list of literature read
3) Have a professor evaluate sample lesson plans and observe a lesson integrating technology

Reflection:
Write a journal entry explaining how technology has improved my teaching effectiveness and student learning

Source: Professional Portfolio of Kate Maczis

Goal II:
To improve my classroom management techniques

Essential Dimensions of Teaching: Standard 6

Action Plan:
1) Observe at least three teachers' different classroom management styles and strategies
2) Seek out management strategies through the Internet, professional magazines and journals
3) Try at least three new techniques during my instruction

Professional Development Plan

Documentation:
1) Create a file of effective classroom management techniques used by other teachers and gathered from research efforts
2) Create a chart showing which techniques were or were not successful and why

Reflection:
Write a journal entry reflecting what I have learned as a result of researching and implementing new techniques for classroom management

Source: Professional Portfolio of Kate Maczis

FIGURE 2.5   A portfolio entry representing a professional development plan.

Reviewing Chapter 2

Understanding how professional standards relate to portfolio development is important. Check your understanding of performance standards and portfolio development by answering the following questions.

What is the most convincing reason for you to use performance standards/themes when developing your portfolio?

_____

_____

What set of performance standards/themes will you select as a foundation for your portfolio? What is your rationale for this selection?

_____

_____

Which specific performance standards/themes are most directly related to your coursework or teaching?

_____

_____

Which specific performance standards/themes are most directly related to your professional development plans?

_____

_____

The next several chapters discuss the three phases of portfolio development: *getting started*, *enhancing your documents*, and *using your portfolio*. These three phases provide a step-by-step method for working through the entire process of portfolio development from beginning to end. Teachers will want to review all three phases each time a new portfolio is created or an existing portfolio is modified for a different purpose.

3 Phase I—Getting Started

THE PORTFOLIO DEVELOPMENT PROCESS can be overwhelming. Many teachers have difficulty making decisions about how to begin this process and where to go next. The "getting started" phase of portfolio development will not only help you get through this road block but will also provide the foundation for all the remaining phases. There are three main tasks involved in Phase I: *determining the purpose of your portfolio*; *considering a set of standards*; and *collecting, selecting, and creating documents*. Understanding and working through these three tasks will help to eliminate some of the anxiety associated with beginning this rigorous endeavor.

Determining the Purpose

To determine the purpose of your portfolio, you will need to review the types of portfolios described in Chapter 1: entrance, working, exit, interview, or showcase portfolio. Each type will require a different kind of decision making regarding the selection of documents and the way in which you present them. If you are creating a portfolio that does not fit into the types defined in this handbook, you need to clarify your purpose and create a portfolio that is appropriate to your situation. Once you know why you are creating your portfolio, you will be able to select portfolio documents relevant to your purpose.

Considering a Set of Performance Standards

Much attention has been given to the importance of considering performance standards in the development of a professional portfolio. As stated in Chapter 2, standards and themes provide a credible theoretical foundation for the collection of your documentation. Teacher candidates will most likely consider a set of standards identified by their teacher preparation program. Inservice teachers will consider national or local standards identified by their individual school or school district. Both teacher candidates and inservice teachers may consider standards identified by their specific subject or specialty area. If your teacher education program or school system does not prescribe a particular set of standards, you will need to review sets of standards on your own.

Appendix A contains selected examples of national standards. Appendix B is a listing of national organizations that have developed professional standards for their members. You might also consider the use of the generic themes suggested in this handbook since they correlate with key performances articulated in many of the standards. Whichever performance standards or themes you select, your documentation should provide evidence of growth and competency related to those standards or themes.

Collecting, Selecting, and Creating Documents

The next task in this phase involves the collection or creation of artifacts to support your portfolio purpose. There are many items that could be included in your portfolio. Having too many documents may create an unwieldy task for the reviewer. The key is to be highly selective by sorting out the best from the rest. Choose only those items that are critical and essential to the purpose of your portfolio. In general, *current artifacts* will have more value than those that represent experiences from many years ago. However, you may include major honors or awards you earned earlier in your career that are still significant regardless of when they were received.

The following examples of portfolio artifacts are organized using *themes* that are inherent in many sets of national, state, or local standards: *Knowledge of Subject Matter, Planning, Delivery and Assessment of Instruction, Classroom Management and Organization, Human Relationship Skills,* and *Professional Qualities.* As you review the ideas for documentation, remember that these examples are relevant to any set of standards and may be helpful to get you started in thinking about what to include in your portfolio. Many of these ideas may apply to more than one standard or theme and should be placed in the portfolio where they are most appropriate.

Suggestions for Portfolio Documentation

If you were to document a standard that relates to your *Knowledge of Subject Matter*, you might include the following artifacts in your portfolio:

- Highlights of a unit of instruction or research paper, reflection on your learning, and implications for future classroom instruction.
- A description of your travel with pictures and an explanation of how this experience contributed to your knowledge of subject matter and how it was applied to classroom instruction.
- Transcripts or descriptions of courses, workshops, study groups, and

staff development experiences that enhanced knowledge of subject matter and/or theory.

- Original materials developed (books, papers, articles) that demonstrate knowledge of subject matter.
- A general reflection about your level of mastery of subject matter.
- Test results that show your competency in content areas; NTE, PRAXIS.
- Notes, letters, written feedback from other professionals regarding your subject matter competency.
- An explanation of how your knowledge of subject matter has informed your instructional decisions, improved your teaching effectiveness, and increased student learning.

All standards include aspects of *Planning, Delivery, and Assessment of Instruction*. Here are some ideas that might be appropriate for documenting your competencies in these areas:

- A reflection on your beliefs about teaching and learning.
- An overview of a long-range unit of instruction.
- An explanation of how you use knowledge of the learner to plan instruction.
- Sample lesson plans.
- An explanation of how you modify instruction to meet the needs of all students.
- Pictures with captions of students engaged in a learning activity.
- A videotape demonstrating your teaching with a written explanation of what is on the video and your analysis of the instruction.
- A web illustrating your repertoire of strategies used for instruction, a rationale for selection of these strategies, and results of instruction.
- A list of strategies used to create a multicultural perspective.
- Samples of student work.
- Samples of assessment tools used to diagnose learning needs.
- Samples of rubrics used to assess student performance.
- A written "think aloud" about your decisions regarding the use of assessment results to diagnose and plan further instruction.
- A chart illustrating before and after assessment of student learning.
- Documentation of how you use technology for planning, delivery, and assessment.
- Pictures of bulletin boards, plays, special events, special projects, field trips, and guest speakers with captions explaining what occurred.
- A professional development plan for increasing effectiveness in planning, delivery, and assessment of instruction.
- Results of solicited feedback from students regarding your effectiveness as a teacher.
- Notes or written feedback from an administrator, supervisor, or cooperating teacher regarding the effectiveness of your instruction.
- A written self-analysis reflecting on your growth in planning, delivery, and assessment of instruction.

Classroom Management and Organization are familiar terms to all educators. However, this terminology is not always used in state and national standards. Classroom management and organization competencies are imbedded throughout many standards. It is obvious that effective classroom management impacts all teaching performance. Therefore, some evidence of your skills and dispositions regarding classroom management should be placed in the portfolio regardless of whether the standards specifically use this term. The examples listed here are some ideas to help you document your competency in this area.

- A statement of your philosophy of classroom management and discipline.
- A description of your policy and procedures for managing your classroom.
- A diagram of the classroom arrangement and explanation of how this arrangement facilitates instruction and management.
- A description of a situation in which you were successful in changing inappropriate student behavior to on-task behavior. Explain what happened and what was learned.
- Pictures of bulletin boards and centers that relate to management and organization of the classroom.
- A description of strategies used for instructional management and/or behavior management.
- A sample of how you keep accurate records (grades, attendance, checklists, progress notes).
- Notes, letters, written feedback regarding the effectiveness of your classroom management.
- A written reflection self-analyzing your classroom management.

How you interact with students, colleagues, parents, and community has a significant impact on your success as a teacher. The state and national standards that are labeled Social Context, Social Development, Family Outreach, Family Partnerships, and Collaboration with Colleagues each include performances that require effective *Human Relationships*. Here are a few examples of documents that could support these categories.

- A letter of introduction or newsletter written by you to the parents of your students or school community.
- An explanation of special strengths you have in creating positive working relationships with students, other teachers, parents, administrators, and supervisors.
- A description of experiences working with diversity in the classroom and what you do to make all students feel included.
- What you do to involve the broader educational community in the instructional program for students.

- A document or graphic organizer that explains or shows what you have done to enhance collaboration with colleagues.
- Notes and letters from students, parents, school, or university professionals regarding your interpersonal skills.
- A reflective entry describing your interpersonal style of developing positive and productive working relationships.

Professionalism can be documented by including any artifact that demonstrates your commitment to the profession. The examples below are some ways to document professionalism:

- A current professional development plan
- A current résumé
- A list of memberships in professional organizations
- A description of leadership positions held
- Evidence of degrees, honors, awards, and recognition received
- Evidence of your volunteer work, special projects, programs, and participation on committees related to education
- Research, articles, papers written or co-authored
- Letters from administrators commenting on your professional qualities: responsibility, reliability, punctuality, attitude, etc.
- Evaluations
- A written statement of your goals for future professional growth

If you choose to include photographs and/or a videotape in your portfolio, you will need to secure permission from a parent or legal guardian to use these documents. See Appendix D for a sample letter of permission and Appendix E for additional information related to including a videotape in your portfolio.

These examples of portfolio documents are provided to stimulate your thinking and are by no means exhaustive. Consider these ideas as you collect, select, and create your portfolio artifacts. Please see Appendix F for a worksheet to help you think about what you already have and what you need in order to begin the collection of documents for your portfolio. The final selection of materials for your portfolio will be based on the purpose of the portfolio, the audience, and your personal preferences for documentation.

Reviewing Chapter 3

The information in this chapter was intended to help you begin the process of portfolio development. Use these questions to focus your thinking about what you need to do to get started.

What is the purpose of your portfolio?

_____

_____

Which set of standards or themes will you select to provide a credible, theoretical foundation for selection of your portfolio documents?

_____

_____

What artifacts will you collect or create for your portfolio to provide authentic and convincing evidence of your competency as a teacher?

_____

_____

Now that you have clarified your purpose, considered the use of standards or themes, and become aware of the multitude of artifacts that can be included to demonstrate your teaching effectiveness, you are ready to learn how to enhance this documentation.

4 Phase II—Enhancing Your Documents

EACH CHAPTER IN THIS HANDBOOK has attempted to increase your understanding of the concept and process of portfolio development. This chapter is no different. However, the emphasis in this chapter is twofold. It will present the enhancing your documents phase and its components as well as a section entitled *Turning a Teaching Experience into a Portfolio Entry*, which will help you apply all that you have learned thus far.

The enhancing your documents phase of portfolio development is one of the most crucial phases in this process. The work that you do during this time can make the difference between developing a pretty picture book or a respectable testimonial of your professional accomplishments. This phase has three components: *connecting standards to portfolio documentation, supporting your documents,* and *displaying your documents.*

Most teachers begin to get serious about the enhancement phase when they are preparing their portfolio documents for use in an interview or presentation situation. Regardless of the intent, careful attention to the attributes in this phase will foster the creation of a professional portfolio that will represent you well under most circumstances.

Connecting Standards to Portfolio Documentation

In Phase I you identified a set of standards or themes that informed your decision making in the selection of portfolio documents. In essence, each document that you create or select should support your competency in meeting the performance identified in the standard or theme. You will need to communicate to the portfolio reviewer the relationship between your documentation and performance standards. One of the most effective methods for achieving this is to create a chart that cross-references your artifacts with the performance standards or themes. The portfolio reviewer can see at a glance the relationship between the standards or themes and your artifacts. The following charts have been presented to help you understand the concept of cross-referencing standards with portfolio artifacts. Consider including one of these organizational formats in your portfolio. The chart in Figure 4.1, on page 30, provides further credibility to your documentation.

Furthermore, it is possible that the reviewer may be specifically looking for your ability to integrate standards with your portfolio content.

Artifacts and Standards Cross-Reference Chart

Portfolio Artifacts	INTASC Performance Standards									
	1	2	3	4	5	6	7	8	9	10
Philosophy of Education	*	*			*					
Lesson Plan (Mathematics)							*			
Unit Plan Social Studies				*			*	*		
Sample Tests								*		
Student Work			*							
Behavior Management Plan					*					
Professional Development Plan								*		

See Chapter 7 for actual portfolio artifacts from teacher candidates who used these formats.

Standards and Artifacts Cross-Reference Chart

Performance Standard/Theme	Artifacts
Knowledge of Subject Matter	Research paper Transcripts Honor Society award Praxis score
Planning Delivery and Assessment of Instruction	Lesson/Unit Plans Sample Tests/Student Work Videotape Observational Feedback and Evaluations
Family and Community Relationship	Letters to parents Letters from parents School newsletter Special projects
Classroom Management	Classroom rules Case study Seating arrangement Reflection

FIGURE 4.1 Cross-reference charts.

Supporting Your Documents

Most instructional artifacts cannot stand alone. Narratives need to be provided for the portfolio reviewer to fully understand the significance of each item included in your portfolio and its relevance to your teaching competencies. Writing meaningful introductions, clear explanations, and insightful reflections provides this type of information and support for the documents you are presenting. Therefore, it is important that you give careful attention to how you communicate your thoughts in each of these informative entries.

Introductions

Introductions are narratives that are usually found at the *beginning* of the portfolio or at the onset of each *new section*. The intent of an introduction is to provide an overview of the forthcoming material. An introduction, which occurs in the beginning of the portfolio, often includes the purpose of the portfolio and a philosophy of education. The introduction can also include an overview of the standards or themes that are being used, a rationale for the inclusion of the documents, and an organizational chart cross-referencing documents with standards. Section introductions may include some of the same type of information.

Explanations

Explanations are narratives that provide information about the artifacts presented. They provide a better understanding of each document that cannot be captured by the artifact alone. An explanation can include a rationale for the selection of the document, a description of the event, and the teacher/student learning outcomes resulting from the experience. Explanations should be placed throughout the entire portfolio. They can range from a *full page* to a *short caption* connected to a photograph or other entry. Some artifacts, such as transcripts, résumés, and letters of recommendation, are self-explanatory and do not need an explanation. Most artifacts, however, are enhanced by including an explanation. One way to determine if you need an explanation is to have someone review your portfolio. If they have difficulty understanding the relevance of the documents, then an explanation is needed.

Reflections

Reflection is a highly complex thinking process that is cultivated over time. It is a process that requires careful and analytical thinking about issues related to the teaching profession. Typically, reflection involves systematically and insightfully thinking about what you are doing and the effects of your instruction on student behavior and achievement. The intent of reflection is to develop the ongoing awareness of a teacher's own thoughts, feelings, teaching decisions, and student reactions. It should lead to insightful change of behavior toward the improvement of instruction and the increased probability of student learning.

Portfolio reflective entries are written thoughts, feelings, insights, and questions that represent your personal analysis of professional issues. Written reflections may communicate to the portfolio reviewer information about how you make teaching decisions, how you apply theory to classroom practice, how your teaching has made a difference in the lives of students and the goals of the school, and how you intend to increase your teaching effectiveness and student learning.

When actual teaching artifacts are combined with reflections, the reviewer begins to understand the thought processes that result in decisions that shape the teacher's actions and promote growth. Reflections allow the reviewer to gain insight to teacher decision making and learning that resulted from the event or instructional situation. They bring meaning to artifacts and demonstrate your ability to analyze your performance and growth from an experience. When explanations and reflections are part of one document, they provide the reviewer with information about what occurred as well as your insights related to the teaching and learning experience.

Writing about your thoughts, feelings, and insights may be a difficult task for some individuals. The sentence starters in Figure 4.2 will facilitate your thinking and help you to get started in writing reflective entries for your portfolio. These are only a few ways to begin a reflective entry. Each individual's reflective entries will be unique to his or her specific experiences, writing style, and own way of processing those experiences.

Figure 4.3, on page 34, shows how one teacher combined introductions, explanations, and reflections in a single portfolio entry. This entry is part of a larger set of artifacts that documents the teacher's science program. Chapter 7 includes additional examples of artifacts with introductions, explanations, and reflections from a variety of portfolios.

Displaying Your Documents

Blending the elements of an appealing visual display with meaningful documents is a key element in enhancing your portfolio. Up to this point you have concentrated on collecting and developing high quality artifacts that reflect the complexities of teaching and your competence as a teacher. This component requires you to make decisions on how you will represent these entries on each page of your portfolio. The decisions you make in how to display your portfolio documentation will highly influence the way in which your work is perceived by the reviewer. The main idea is to have artifacts with significance and substance that are displayed in a professional manner. There are three areas for decision making during this component: *housing the contents, organizing the documents,* and *formatting individual entries.*

- *I know that my teaching has increased student learning because …*
- *What I have learned from this experience is …*
- *After observing my students, I realized …*
- *What I think I will do differently is …*
- *When I considered what happened, I …*
- *As a result of this activity, I now …*
- *A real eye opener for me is …*
- *The most significant learning for me was …*
- *After carefully considering …, I think …*
- *This experience has helped me to understand …*
- *I have noticed that …*
- *Since I have … I feel …*
- *I have gained significant growth in the areas of … due to …*
- *Some of the areas that I need to continue to gain experience are … because …*
- *I have gained considerable insight about …*
- *In assessing my own performance I …*
- *I strongly believe …*
- *When I think about …, I realize …*
- *A new learning for me …*
- *In order for me to continue to grow …*
- *I now understand the importance of …*
- *Some questions that still remain in my mind are …*
- *My goals for future professional growth are …*

FIGURE 4.2   Sentence starters for reflective entries.

Housing

Housing the contents is the simplest of these decisions. Choosing something small and easy to carry, such as a loose-leaf notebook, seems to work well for most people. A loose-leaf notebook provides the flexibility to add, remove, or reorganize the documentation as needed. For example, items from one type of portfolio can be fine-tuned or adapted

Observation of a Social System

Inquiry Focus: What fosters science learning?

Introduction: Twice a week for eleven weeks, I observed, participated, and designed several learning events in a second grade classroom at a local school. Based on the data collected from observations of teacher-student, student-student, and individual interactions, as well as the learning environment, I was able to collect several thoughts about science learning.

Journal Part One:
Context of Science Learning

The students designed and implemented their own experiment to observe what makes objects sink or float. They used their observations to conjuncture what attributes determined whether an object sinks or floats.

Journal Part Two:
Articulation of Thoughts and Conjectures

It was very interesting to observe the students actually look for what motivated them during this lesson. Was it playing with water, doing science, talking among themselves about their observations, or solving the mystery of what makes objects sink or float? I think it was a little of everything, but I especially think the challenge was a large motivating factor. The main idea focused on *discovering* what determines when an object sinks or floats. The students were challenged each step of the way with contradicting questions and demonstrations that provided evidence that one theory could not be true. It became almost a game to determine who would conjecture the right attribute. There were no rewards established, other than the satisfaction of solving the mystery, or being the only person to have an idea that could not be challenged with a demonstration

Explanation: I documented these science learning observations in weekly reflective journals. These journals were organized in two parts. The first detailed the context and environment of the science learning event, as well as what occurred. In the second part, I analyzed and articulated my thoughts and conjectures about what fostered science learning

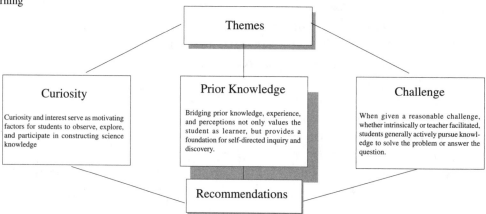

Themes

Curiosity

Curiosity and interest serve as motivating factors for students to observe, explore, and participate in constructing science knowledge

Prior Knowledge

Bridging prior knowledge, experience, and perceptions not only values the student as learner, but provides a foundation for self-directed inquiry and discovery.

Challenge

When given a reasonable challenge, whether intrinsically or teacher facilitated, students generally actively pursue knowledge to solve the problem or answer the question.

Recommendations

◊   Classroom environments should be filled with tools necessary to investigate the objects and processes of the natural world. Students should be provided with the freedom to observe these objects and answer their own questions or follow their own curiosities.

◊   Conversations should be an integral part of science instruction. The sharing of ideas in a social context allows children to build their own theories based on several perspectives and prior experiences.

◊   Science learning activities should include game like features of chance, discovery, and active use of all thinking skills in order to provide students with the context to be problem solvers, detectives, and investigators. There should be an element of a reasonable challenge, with a strong chance of student success.

Reflection: This experience reinforced my belief about the value of observation and reflection. As an educator, I believe it is my responsibility to be aware of the learners in my classroom community. By conducting disciplined inquiries about the factors that foster learning, I am better equipped to develop learning activities that are more meaningful and authentic for my students. While I was already aware that enticing student curiosity is a motivating factor in lessons, documenting events that demonstrated this notion proved support for this hypothesis.

Source: Professional Portfolio of Rosanna Calabrese

FIGURE 4.3   Combining introductions, explanations, and reflections in one portfolio entry.

for inclusion in a portfolio used for another purpose. However, some people have used file crates, book bags, and other creative ways to present their work. Select the housing appropriate to your purpose and individual style. Many teachers have found that inserting each entry into a clear plastic sheet protector prevents the documents from getting soiled or torn and makes it easier to turn the pages.

Organizing

You will need to make a decision about how to organize and categorize the documents in your portfolio. This decision will be unique to you, the purpose of your portfolio, and the types of documents you have collected. Some individuals have organized their portfolio around standards, themes, artifacts, content areas, goals, or other categories unique to their purpose. A table of contents is essential to the portfolio regardless of how you choose to organize the documents. Using a table of contents in combination with color-coded section tabs is a logical and highly effective approach to organizing and categorizing your materials. This organizational approach represents your thinking, highlights the main sections of the portfolio, and allows easy access to your artifacts.

Formatting

Formatting your portfolio documents refers to the way in which you arrange the artifacts and accompanying narratives on a single page or set of related pages. Remember, visual literacy is an important consideration when preparing documents of this nature. Visual literacy refers to textures, colors, shapes, pictures, drawings, content placement, and the like. Dull, drab, stylistically monotonous pages of content can present a *boring* script and leave the reader with a similar impression of the writer. When making decisions about formatting your documents, consider the following aspects of visual literacy:

Quantity	• How many documents can be effectively displayed on one page?
Quality	• Are the documents clear, legible, and meaningful?
Variety	• Have you selected different ways to represent your experiences and competencies such as charts, graphic organizers, photographs, student work, and your own original materials?
Arrangement	• Are your documents arranged in a logical order on the same page with careful consideration to spacing and size?
Aesthetics	• Have you considered the use of color, borders, and different styles and sizes of lettering?

Turning a Teaching Experience into a Portfolio Entry

All portfolio entries are a result of your experiences as a teacher. The majority of your experiences will result in portfolio entries that represent your ability to plan, deliver, and assess instruction. In addition, you need to consider other experiences that are also an essential part of the teaching role, such as conducting a parent teacher conference, organizing a field trip, directing a school play, or coordinating a special project. These are only a few examples of the many experiences that a teacher encounters in their career. Most of these experiences can be critical learning and growth opportunities worthy of inclusion in a portfolio. Think through all the experiences that you have had and use the guidelines below to help you turn an experience into a portfolio entry.

These guidelines are directly correlated to the portfolio development process presented in Phases I and II.

- Identify the experience.
- Ask yourself why this experience is worthy of having a place in your portfolio.
  Does it support the purpose of your portfolio?
  Does it support a performance standard or theme?
  Does it support your professional goals?
  Did it contribute to your professional growth and learning?
  Did it increase student achievement?
- Select or create artifacts that represent the experience.
- Make decisions about what to say in your introductions, explanations, and reflections to enhance your documents.
- Determine how to display the documents in your portfolio.

Figure 4.4 is based on the guidelines and illustrates how the experience of conducting a parent/teacher conference can become a portfolio entry. It provides a rationale for inclusion of the experience by citing how it supports INTASC Standards 8 and 10: Assessment Strategies and Relationships with Parents. The artifacts that are noted can be actual documents that represent the preparation, implementation, and analysis of the parent teacher conference. The introduction, explanations, and reflections are narratives that provide critical information regarding the conference, its impact on student progress, parental response, and an analysis of the experience. The accompanying graphic shows in Figure 4.5, on page 38, how a parent conference experience can be displayed in a three-page portfolio entry.

Identify the Experience

Parent, teacher, student conference to discuss student performance

Provide a Rationale for Inclusion

Supports
INTASC 8 & 10

Collect or Create Artifacts

△ Letter arranging conference
△ Organization plan for conference
△ Samples of student work that supported teacher evaluation
△ Copy of report card and written comments

△ Action plan to improve performance
△ Note from parents related to satisfaction with the conference
△ Results of this intervention

Write Introductions, Explanations, Reflections

△ Introduction including the purpose of the conference, rationale for selecting this experience, and how it is related to the selected performance standard(s) or theme
△ Explanation of what occurred
△ Explanation of how the samples of student work supported your assessment of the student's performance
△ Reflections on the process, outcomes, and learning related to your professional competency and growth

FIGURE 4.4 **Using the guidelines to develop a portfolio entry for a parent/teacher/ student conference.**

Introduction ....
....
....
....
....

Conference Appointment Letter	Plan

What Occurred ....
....
....
....
....
....

Report Card

. . . . . . A
. C
. . . . . . F

A	A	C
C	C	F

STUDENT WORK and ASSESSMENT

Explanation..
....
....
....

Action Plan for Improving Performance	Parent Response

Results and Reflection ....
....
....
....
....
....
....
....
....
....

FIGURE 4.5   Template for displaying artifacts related to a parent/teacher/student conference.

Reviewing Chapter 4

The questions below will guide your thinking as you attempt to enhance the quality and the presentation of the artifacts in your portfolio.

How will you communicate the relationship between your documentation and performance standards?

_____

_____

What will you include in the general introduction to your portfolio?

_____

_____

How will you introduce each section of your portfolio?

_____

_____

Where will you include captions or explanations?

_____

_____

Where will you place reflective entries?

_____

_____

How will you house and organize your documentation?

_____

_____

What artifacts will you include in your portfolio that represent experiences other than those related to classroom instruction?

_____

_____

You are now ready to enter the final phase of the portfolio development process. This last phase will prepare you to use your portfolio during an interview, evaluation session, or portfolio presentation event.

5 Phase III—Using Your Portfolio

THERE ARE MANY DIFFERENT SITUATIONS where you will be expected to present a professional portfolio. Chapter 1 briefly identified some of these situations when describing the different types of portfolios. To summarize, the *entrance* portfolio is used to screen applicants for admission to a teacher education program. The *working* portfolio is used to document and evaluate ongoing teaching performance and growth over time. The *exit, interview,* or *showcase* portfolios are used in a presentation or interview for the purpose of program completion, employment, or job advancement. This chapter will focus on how to use your portfolio during an exit, interview, or showcase portfolio presentation.

There are two distinct components to Phase III: *self-evaluating your portfolio* and *presenting your portfolio*. The self-evaluation component is a process designed for use by a teacher to reflect on the overall effectiveness of the portfolio before using it for an interview or presentation. The presentation component identifies several recommendations for using your portfolio during an interview.

Self-Evaluating Your Portfolio

Developing a portfolio is a time-consuming and rigorous process. As you move toward the final product, you will be eager to present your work to others. However, it is in your best interest to first invest some time in evaluating your own work. The self-evaluation process focuses on four major areas:

- Introduction and organization of the portfolio
- Performance standards or themes
- Documentation
- Introductions, explanations, and reflections

These areas directly align with the portfolio development process as described in the preceding chapters. To help guide you through this process, we have developed several questions that address the attributes that promote a quality portfolio. By addressing these questions, you will be able to make decisions that will enhance the substance and presentation of your documents before sharing your portfolio in a more formal setting. Even the best portfolio can benefit from the self-evaluation process.

Evaluating the Introduction and Organization of Your Portfolio

The introduction sets the stage for the content of your portfolio. It is the opening statement that includes information regarding your philosophy of teaching, learning, or leadership. It may also include your professional goals that relate to the purpose of your portfolio. Portfolio organization refers to the way the portfolio is assembled.

- Is my introduction meaningful, informative, and related to the purpose of my portfolio?
- Does my introduction include a strong rationale for inclusion of the selected documents?
- Did I include my philosophy of education?
- Are the contents housed logically?
- Are artifacts organized effectively?
- Are the artifacts easily accessible?
- Did I include a plan for continued professional development?

Evaluating Your Use of Performance Standards, Themes, or Goals

Performance standards identify the knowledge, dispositions, and skills that a teacher should know and be able to demonstrate. They provide the conceptual framework for portfolio development and documentation. *Goals* identify areas for professional development and correlate with performance standards or themes. *Themes* are generic categories that are inherent throughout the performance standards.

- Are performance-based standards, themes, or goals used as the foundation for my portfolio documentation?
- Is there evidence in my portfolio that communicates how I have used standards, goals, or themes?
- Did I include a cross-reference chart?

Evaluating Your Documentation

Documentation refers to the artifacts selected to support your professional competencies. They may be a combination of teacher-made materials, student work, evaluation documents completed by others that validate your professional performance, and additional materials as appropriate to the purpose of the portfolio.

- Are all my artifacts relevant to the purpose?
- Are my artifacts directly related to a standard(s),theme(s), or goal(s)?
- Do the artifacts provide substantial evidence in support of my competency and growth toward that standard(s), theme(s), or goal(s)?
- Do I have a variety of artifacts organized thoughtfully and displayed effectively?
- Are my artifacts accompanied by introductions, explanations, and reflections?

- Are my evaluative documents current and completed by professionals who have first-hand knowledge of my performance?
- Do my artifacts show significant evidence to support student learning and/or the results of my instruction?

Evaluating Your Introductions, Explanations, and Reflections

Introductions, explanations, and reflections are narrative entries that provide information about the documents and insight about the portfolio developer's thoughts related to teaching and learning.

- Are my introductions at the beginning of each section clearly articulated, and do they provide a rationale for inclusion of the forthcoming documents, linkage to my philosophical beliefs, and comments about how the documents support the standard, theme or goal?
- Do my explanations clearly describe the document and its relevance to the standard, goal, theme, or purpose of my portfolio?
- Do my explanations provide other information to help the reviewer understand how this entry supports my ability to teach, impact student learning, or demonstrate leadership?
- Do my reflections provide evidence of my ability to think critically, problem solve, make decisions, relate theory to practice, learn from experience, and/or grow professionally?

To complement the information just presented, we have designed a worksheet to structure the self-evaluation process (see Appendix G). This worksheet is intended for use by the portfolio developer. However, it could be given to other individuals for their input prior to using your portfolio in an actual interview or presentation.

Now that you have an understanding of how to self-evaluate your portfolio, you need to be aware of the fact that portfolio reviewers will identify specific criteria to evaluate your documentation. Being aware of this criteria will help you further assess the effectiveness of your own portfolio and be better prepared to use your portfolio during an interview.

Appendix H contains an example of an overall portfolio assessment instrument developed by the authors. This instrument includes criteria that may be used by individuals who are evaluating your performance and are reviewing your portfolio documents. It is a Likert scale that rates ten essential aspects of the portfolio on a continuum from 1–5. This comprehensive, generic assessment tool is intended to help you to evaluate the overall quality of the portfolio. You may give this to a peer, colleague, professor, or administrator to use in a practice portfolio presentation or mock interview.

Appendix I provides examples of actual guidelines and rubrics used by two teacher education programs: Villa Julie College and George Mason University. The guidelines identify the required portfolio contents and the rubrics identify the criteria used to evaluate the documentation. This information may be useful for individuals who are interested in seeing how teacher education programs implement the portfolio development process and evaluate portfolio documentation.

Presenting Your Portfolio

The presentation of your portfolio is the culminating component in the portfolio development process. It is the point at which teachers share their portfolios for the purpose of gaining employment or supporting career enhancement. The portfolio, in this phase, is a carefully selected collection of exemplary documents that highlight a teacher's best work and accomplishments.

Presented below are some helpful hints drawn from many conversations with teacher candidates, inservice teachers, administrators, and personnel directors about their first-hand experiences with the use of portfolios during interviews. While these helpful hints are geared to the job interviews, they can apply to other portfolio presentation situations. Keeping these suggestions in mind can dramatically improve the quality of your professional interview with personnel staff and/or school administrators.

1. **Bring your portfolio to all interviews.** Be ready to present your portfolio at every interview. Let the interviewer know that you have brought your portfolio with you and would appreciate the opportunity to share portions of it. Be aware that you may not have the option of sharing your portfolio during large-scale interview situations where many teachers are tightly scheduled. However, you should still have your portfolio with you. Some interviewers are very impressed by the effort you devoted to preparing this product and they will at least glance through it and make a notation that you have developed a professional teaching portfolio.

2. **Be prepared to present your portfolio to the principal.** Most teachers have found that they are more likely to have the opportunity to share their portfolio during a one-on-one interview with the school principal. In fact, many administrators expect to see a portfolio at this time. This interview is typically longer and more personalized with sufficient time to review your portfolio. Both teacher candidates and inservice teachers claimed that their portfolios were a critical aspect of this more personal interview. Be prepared to present your portfolio during this type of interview.

3. **Know the location of your documents.** Be familiar with the organization of your portfolio so that when the opportunity presents itself you can locate an example of your work without searching frantically through the contents. The use of a detailed table of contents with color-coded tabs for each portfolio section will assist you in locating artifacts quickly.

Know the contents of your portfolio well so that you can unobtrusively work your portfolio into the interview. There will be times during the interview when a question is asked that directly relates to one or more of your portfolio documents. Take advantage of this situation to bring your portfolio to the attention of the interviewer. You might say, *Let me show you a document that* . . . Sharing this document may bring more credibility to your response.

4. **Position your portfolio strategically.** Place your portfolio in a position so that it is facing the interviewer. This may mean that you will have to explain your documents from an upside-down view. Practice this maneuver prior to your interview.

5. **Keep your portfolio a reasonable size.** Do not present a massive portfolio. The documents presented in your portfolio should include a limited number of artifacts that can easily be reviewed during the interview time. Be highly selective, including only the most essential documents relevant to the purpose of the interview.

6. **Be sensitive to the interview process.** Do not dominate the interview by sharing your portfolio page by page unless requested by the interviewer. Allow the interviewer to determine the structure of the interview.

7. **Conduct a "mock" interview.** Practice responding to interview questions using your portfolio. If possible, select a classmate or colleague to role play the interview with you. Rehearsing prior to the real interview may build your self-confidence and facilitate a smooth transition from the interviewer's question to your response to sharing a portfolio entry. Identify the portfolio documents that directly relate to or support your response to the typical interview questions posed here.
   - What is your philosophy of education?
   - What are your *best practices* in the area of classroom management and discipline?
   - What strategies have you found to be most effective in teaching (*insert subject here*)?
   - How do you promote productive working relationships with parents, colleagues, and community?
   - How do you deal with difficult parents?
   - What are your most effective motivational strategies?
   - What methods of assessment do you use to determine student learning?
   - What do you consider to be your strengths or areas for continued growth?
   - Tell me about your involvement in professional projects, activities, or organizations related to teaching.

8. **Leave a small sampling of your documents.** Create a small version of your portfolio that you can give to the interviewer. Some principals may ask you to leave your portfolio with them so that they can take more time to review its contents. If this is not something that you feel comfortable doing, prepare a small sampling of documents that can be left with the interviewer. Consider including your *philosophy*, a

lesson plan with a *reflection about your teaching effectiveness and student learning,* a *current résumé,* a *recent evaluation,* and one or two *letters of recommendation.*

In summary, evaluating the effectiveness of your portfolio and practicing how to use your portfolio are two of the most valuable activities you can engage in to prepare yourself for your portfolio presentation or interview.

Reviewing Chapter 5

Consider these questions as you prepare to use your portfolio.

What did you learn from using the portfolio self-evaluation chart?

_____

_____

What improvements will you need to make to increase the effectiveness of your portfolio?

_____

_____

What did you learn from participating in a mock interview?

_____

_____

How will you incorporate your learning into a real interview?

_____

_____

What will you include in your small packet of portfolio documents to leave with the reviewer?

_____

_____

You have now learned about the entire process of portfolio development. This process is applicable to the development of both a paper-based portfolio or an electronic portfolio. The next chapter will provide a general overview of electronic portfolios so that you may consider this as an alternative to a paper-based portfolio.

6 Electronic Portfolios: An Option

WITH THE MAJOR TREND toward the use of technology in school systems and higher education, and the development of national standards for technology, many teachers and teacher candidates are being encouraged to consider an electronic portfolio as an alternative to a paper-based portfolio. According to recent literature (Barrett, 1999; Goldsby & Fazal, 2000; Jackson, 1997; McKinney, 1998), teachers who can demonstrate their technological competence through an electronic portfolio have an advantage in securing a teaching position and are more likely to incorporate technology into their own classroom.

Although most portfolios are developed with a computer and require some technological knowledge and skills, electronic portfolios require a more sophisticated understanding of the programs and processes related to this multimedia approach. Because the task of developing an electronic portfolio can appear to be intimidating, it is important to understand what is involved before moving in this direction.

The intent of this chapter is to provide:

- A general overview of the process for developing an electronic portfolio.
- A listing of the skills needed to develop an electronic portfolio.
- Information on the variety of the hardware and software necessary to produce an electronic portfolio.
- A list of resources for developing an electronic portfolio.
- Information on the options and issues for publishing an electronic portfolio.

This information should help you to determine if creating an electronic portfolio is a realistic option for you. The portfolio development concept and process presented in the previous chapters of this handbook apply to both paper-based and electronic portfolios. The major difference is the technological skills, materials, and equipment you will need to create an electronic presentation.

What Is an Electronic Portfolio?

The electronic portfolio, just like the paper-based portfolio, is a carefully selected collection of exemplary documents that highlights a teacher's best work and accomplishments. However, unlike the paper-based portfolio, the electronic portfolio is a multimedia approach that allows the teacher to present teaching, learning, and reflective artifacts in a variety of formats (audio, video, graphics, and text). Hypermedia links are used to connect standards or goals to artifacts as opposed to section dividers or tabs.

The electronic portfolio, sometimes referred to as a digital or computer-generated portfolio, is typically published on the Internet (World Wide Web, WWW, Web) or on a CD. This type of portfolio requires the reviewer to have access to a computer.

Developing an electronic portfolio brings together the processes of both multimedia project development and portfolio development. These complementary processes are essential for an effective electronic portfolio presentation (Barrett, 2000).

Why Should I Consider Developing an Electronic Portfolio?

Several authors who wrote on the use of electronic portfolios (Ascherman, 1999; Barrett 1999, 2000; Boulware & Holt, 1998; Goldsby & Fazal, 2000; Jackson, 1997; Milman, 1999; Riggsby, Jewell, & Justice, 1995; Wiedmer, 1998) identified the specific benefits of using this approach.

- Technology expertise is now required for beginning teachers. Teachers who can demonstrate their skills in technology have an advantage in acquiring teaching positions.
- Technology competency can be demonstrated through an electronic portfolio.
- Teachers who develop an electronic portfolio will be more likely to infuse technology into their classroom, requiring their own students to develop electronic portfolios.
- Electronic portfolios allow clear and immediate connections between standards and portfolio artifacts through hypertext links.
- An electronic portfolio that is published on the WWW is widely accessible and easily distributed to a large number of people.
- A portfolio published on the Internet will provide the opportunity to receive immediate feedback from any reviewer via an email link.
- An Internet-based portfolio and can be revised whenever necessary.
- CD portfolios are easily duplicated.
- Electronic portfolios have a large storage capacity and multiple modality presentation options.
- Electronic portfolios allow beginning teachers to market their skills or strengths in a more professional and compelling manner.
- Portfolio reviewers can experience a multimedia presentation. They can watch a lesson, hear real student interactions, and listen to a teacher's reflections rather than read about them.

Do I Have the Technological Knowledge and Skills?

The minimum level of knowledge and skills necessary for considering the development of an electronic portfolio is basic computer literacy. Basic computer literacy requires that you understand the fundamentals of computer hardware and software and know how to use a variety of software programs. More specifically, you will need to know how to use your computer to create word processing documents and incorporate computer graphics. If you do not have this basic level of computer literacy, an electronic portfolio presentation will not be a realistic option at this time. Electronic portfolios are not for everyone.

If you consider yourself computer literate and want to develop an electronic portfolio that requires a higher level of skills than you currently have, you should think about taking a course, a workshop, or seeking out a mentor who has this knowledge and expertise. You will also have to consider the time that it will take to develop the skills necessary for this type of presentation. If you think that you have an adequate level of technological knowledge and skills, and you have the time to develop an electronic portfolio, the overview provided in this chapter will assist you in getting started in this process.

What Computer Hardware Will I Need?

The following hardware is suggested to begin the process of creating an electronic portfolio:

- **A computer with**
  - sufficient memory (64 to 128 MB of RAM)
  - video input and output (if you plan to include sound and video in your portfolio)
  - Internet server access (if you plan to publish your portfolio on the Internet)
- **Flat-bed color scanner**
- **Digital camera**
- **Digital video camera** (if you decide to incorporate video clips in your portfolio)
- **CD-RW burner** (if you plan to publish your portfolio on a CD)
- **Zip drive**

Many colleges have computer labs with appropriate hardware and software as well as individuals with technological expertise who are available to help. Most school systems have computer equipment as well as a technology consultant on site or in a central office. Both teacher candidates and practicing teachers have the opportunity to utilize these resources when developing their electronic portfolio.

What Computer Software Will I Need?

The required software can be divided into several categories: hypermedia "card" formats, HTML or web authoring software, multimedia slideshow software, PDF documents, and general utilities. The basis of selection from any of these categories is dependent upon availability of the software, your technological expertise, the purpose of your portfolio, and the type of computer you are using (PC or Macintosh). The following chart shows the most commonly cited electronic portfolio development software for teachers.

Formats	Software
Hypermedia "Card" Programs	
Software programs that allow the integration of graphics, sound, and movies in a single file. Electronic cards or screens are linked together by developer-created buttons.	Digital Chisel HyperStudio Multimedia Toolbook
HTML or Web-Authoring Software	
Software programs that will translate your text and graphics into an HTML format. Web-authoring software will generally allow you to copy and paste word processing text into a web page.	Adobe PageMill Claris HomePage Microsoft FrontPage Macromedia DreamWeaver Netscape Composer
Multimedia Slideshow Software	
Multimedia slideshow software allows the portfolio developer to create electronic slides that incorporate sound and video in a linear sequence.	Adobe Persuasion AppleWorks Microsoft PowerPoint
PDF Documents	
A universal file format that preserves all of the fonts, formatting, colors, and graphics of any source document, regardless of the application and platform used to create it.	Adobe Acrobat
General Utilities	
Software programs that facilitate and enhance the development of an electronic portfolio.	Adobe Photo Deluxe Adobe PhotoShop Clip art and digital photos Paint Shop Pro

Helen Barrett (2000) provides an in-depth analysis of several of these formats, their advantages and disadvantages, and their appropriateness for specific electronic portfolio purposes.

Options and Issues When Publishing an Electronic Portfolio

The two most prevalent options of publishing an electronic portfolio are a CD or the Internet. Before deciding on either of these methods, you will need to be aware of several important issues. Understanding the pros and cons of CD and Internet publication will help you to make the appropriate choice.

Publishing on a CD-ROM

A CD allows you to include 650 MB of text, graphics, video, and sound. CDs are easy to store and duplicate, making it feasible for teachers to distribute multiple copies of a portfolio. Most CD burners produce a CD for either platform, MAC or PC. Additionally, the cost of a blank CD has dropped to approximately $1.00. The cost of a CD burner has also decreased. These factors make the CD a viable option for duplicating the electronic portfolio. A disadvantage to publishing on a CD is the difficulty in updating or changing a portfolio once it has been recorded on the CD. Making changes requires the rewriting or burning of a new CD. You would need access to the appropriate hardware and software to record any changes.

Publishing on the Internet

Publishing on the Internet is limited to the space available to you on a Web server. When teacher candidates graduate, they will lose their space on the university or college's Web server. Similarly, teachers who store their Web page on a school system server will also lose that space if they change school systems. Teachers must decide if they want to purchase space on a commercial site or utilize free space, which includes a lot of irrelevant advertising that may distract the viewer from the substance of the portfolio presentation.

An Internet-based electronic portfolio can be accessed any time by anyone with on-line capability. Barrett (1999, 2000) raises the issue that publishing a portfolio on the Web can inhibit the quality of reflection. Since it will be accessible to the public, will the portfolio developer provide thoughtful, personal reflection when many have access to his or her most private thoughts? Ascherman (1999) raises this issue as well. Several of his students strenuously objected to having personal data, letters of recommendations, evaluations, and so on in the public domain or on all computers in the world (p. 4). Individuals can password protect their portfolio contents by providing their password only to portfolio reviewers. To further ensure confidentiality, delete personal data, yours or others, that should not be accessible to the public, such as names, addresses, phone numbers, and social security numbers.

Since the Internet is accessible to so many people, an individual's intellectual property rights can be threatened. Documents on the Web can be copied and used by others. There is little you can do to ensure that this will not happen.

In addition, teachers who choose to include artifacts such as photographs of their students, letters of recommendations, or other similar document types must be sure to secure permission for including these items in their portfolio. Copyright laws must be adhered to if you use clip art, digital photos, or other commercially prepared material.

Regardless of whether a portfolio is published on the Internet or CD-ROM, the developer needs to be aware of a tendency to include the *bells and whistles* that are so readily available. Try to avoid this temptation. As with the paper-based portfolio, the substance, not the packaging, of the portfolio is paramount.

The choice of publishing an electronic portfolio via the Internet or CD-ROM is clearly an important decision. It can only be made after careful consideration of your individual preferences, your situation, and the hardware and software available to you. Most electronic portfolio development software can be used to publish on either a CD-ROM or the Internet. Keep in mind that the portfolio reviewer needs to have the necessary hardware and software to access your electronic portfolio. Being aware of this dilemma will help you to determine whether to develop a paper-based or electronic portfolio. If you develop both types, then you will surely be prepared for any situation. Using PDF software will allow you to publish your portfolio in both an electronic and paper-based format.

Where Can I Get Additional Information and See Actual Examples?

Although there are a number of articles in professional journals, there are not many complete guides that describe how to develop an electronic portfolio. At the time of this publication, the best source of information was available on the Internet. Use of the popular search engines such as AskJeeves, Google, Northernlight, and others will provide links to valuable information. Using a public or university library access to search the ERIC databases will provide another way to access information in the form of articles and research papers about electronic portfolios.

In addition, there are many sites that contain portfolio examples, helpful hints, and information specific to the K–12 sector. This information can be adapted for use by teachers to create their own electronic portfolios as well as assist them in incorporating electronic portfolios for students in their own classroom.

The authors found several particularly helpful higher education sites that provided examples and resources for electronic portfolio development. These were:

- University of Virginia's Curry School of Education
  http://curry.edschool.virginia.edu/curry//class//edlf/589_004/sample.html
- Virginia Tech Teacher Education in the Sciences and Humanities (TESH)
  http://www.tandl.vt.edu/TESH
- Missouri Western State College
  http://www.mwsc.edu/~educatn/ascherport.html
- Webster University School of Education
  http://owl.webster.edu/eportfolio/resources.html
- The Portfolio Development Web Site of Dr. Helen Barrett, University of Alaska
  http://transition.alaska.edu/www/portfolios/bookmarks.html/#teach

Helpful Hints

Much of the best advice comes from individuals who have had first-hand experiences in developing electronic portfolios. Israel Elder, a student at Missouri Western State College, has published his advice to potential electronic portfolio developers (http://www.mwsc.edu/~edexp/studentview2.html). Most of these helpful hints are applicable to either a CD-ROM or Internet-based portfolio. Below is a summary of his comments.

1. **Keep each page short.** Interest is lost when a page contains only text and is too long. Use short paragraphs with space between them.
2. **Use hyperlinks.** Instead of creating one long page, use links to other pages. This requires more work for the developer but is more appealing and convenient for accessing your documents.
3. **Make each page user friendly.** If your reviewers are novices on the computer, and your organizational system too complex, they may become frustrated and will not take the time to access your information.
4. **Keep it simple.** If you choose to include the "bells and whistles," remember there is a huge disparity among Internet connections and transfer rates. Downloading a page full of pictures or graphics may take a long time depending on the Web connection. Using special effects also affects the quality of the page, text fonts, and size of page.
5. **Trial viewing.** View your portfolio from several different computers using different Web browsers and locations. By doing this you can pick up problems in loading time, size of font, and quality of colors.
6. **Independent viewers.** Getting opinions from others will provide the opportunity to make constructive changes before publishing on the Web.

7. **Push your page.** If you have published your portfolio on the Web, put your Web address on your resume. Be sure to let potential employers know that you have a Web page, and, if necessary, show them how to access your page.

It is obvious that the trend toward increased use of technology in the schools and improved computer literacy among students and teachers is having a profound impact on teacher education. As the power and availability of technology increases and the costs of hardware and software decrease, teachers will be forced to expand their knowledge and skills to keep up with the technological standards for the profession. Jackson (1997) believes that "In the future, the question educators will be asking themselves isn't if they should utilize electronic portfolios, but how they should utilize them" (p. 700).

Making the decision to develop an electronic portfolio is certainly in keeping with this current and continuing trend. While it is exciting to think about the potential benefits of implementing this emerging form of technology, it is also important to understand the amount of technological knowledge and skills needed as well as the issues that affect the development and publication of an electronic portfolio (Georgi & Crowe, 1998). If you plunge into this activity without the essential technological literacy, appropriate hardware and software, readily accessible support, and the time needed to prepare a product of this magnitude, you could be setting yourself up for a very frustrating experience .

This chapter has given you introductory information to be able to make an informed decision about whether you should consider developing an electronic portfolio. Keep in mind that regardless of whether you decide on a paper-based or electronic portfolio, the substance and credibility of the documentation (artifacts and reflections) are more important than the format in which you choose to present your work.

Reviewing Chapter 6

Now that you have an overview of the concept of electronic portfolios and have decided that you want to develop one, answering the following questions will help you to get started.

Do you need to obtain any further technological knowledge or skills before beginning this process?

_____

_____

What hardware and software are available to you?

_____

_____

Where will you get the support you may need to complete this process?

_____

_____

Which computer software best suits your purpose and level of technological skill? What is your rationale for this selection?

_____

_____

Which publication method will you select (CD-ROM or Internet)? Provide a rationale for your selection.

_____

_____

The final chapter includes samples of artifacts from the professional portfolios of novice and experienced teachers. They are included to help you see the many ways you can represent your teaching experiences and organize your documentation. All examples can be represented in either paper-based or electronic portfolios.

7 Examples of Portfolio Entries

About This Chapter

This chapter is filled with examples of portfolio documents that are representative of the many ways you can present your professional experiences and accomplishments. The entries have been selected from elementary and secondary teachers' portfolios. Many of them include reflections, explanations, or captions to support the artifacts. Those artifacts that do not have explanations or reflections are included to provide ideas for types of artifacts to consider. Several of the examples include pictures of students. Due to issues of confidentiality, we were not able to publish those original photographs. A camera icon has been used to denote where a photograph was placed.

Portfolio entries such as letters from parents, students, supervisors and administrators, samples of certificates and awards, transcripts, test scores, and written evaluations have intentionally been omitted. These are documents that speak for themselves and do not require a lot of creativity on your part. However, they are an important part of your portfolio and should be included in your documentation.

The examples are grouped into two parts: *introductory artifacts* and *instructional artifacts*. The introductory artifacts include items that address the content and organization of the portfolio. The instructional artifacts include a variety of examples from teachers' portfolios that represent many aspects of teaching. All of the examples selected are intended to stimulate your thinking about different and creative ways to represent your teaching experiences in your professional portfolio. Keep in mind that there is no right or wrong way to present your work. Every portfolio is a product that reflects the uniqueness of the individual creating it.

Examples of Introductory Artifacts

Contents

1	**Knowledge of Content and Educational Theory**
2	**Planning, Delivery and Assessment of Instruction**
3	**Classroom Management and Organization**
4	**Human Relationship Skills**
5	**Professional Qualities**

It is essential to include a table of contents at the beginning of your portfolio. It presents the organizational framework of your artifacts. The example on the left identifies the main categories used to organize the portfolio. The examples below are section dividers with color-coded tabs that correlate with the categories in the table of contents. Tabs allow easy access to the artifacts in each section. They are particularly helpful during an interview when you need to quickly locate an example which supports your response to a question.

Classroom Management and Organization

Human Relationship Skills

Contents

Personal Documents

- Resume
- Philosophy of Education
- Praxis Documentation
- Graphic Organizer of Courses Taken
- Official Transcript
- Professional Recommendations

Evidence of Planning

- Introduction
- Monthly Unit Plan
- Weekly Lesson Plan
- Daily Lesson Plan
- Classroom Activities
  - Stock Purchasing Game
  - Political Cartoon Project and Student Work
  - Letter of Complaint Project
- Check Writing Project
- Formative Evaluation
- Summative Evaluation

Instructional Delivery

- Introduction
- Didactic Teaching
- Cooperative Learning
  - Silent Work
- Working with Small Groups
- Use of Secondary Sources
- Graphic Organizers
- Use of the Computer in Instruction

Classroom Management

- Introduction
- Philosophy on Discipline
- Elements of Motivation
- Classroom Layouts
- Student Responses
- Professionalism in the Classroom
- Working with Adolescents
- Classroom Rules

Supporting Materials

Conclusion

Source: Professional Portfolio of Scott Mooney

These examples of tables of contents include a listing of all items in each section of the portfolio. The portfolio reviewer can see at a glance the types of artifacts that have been included to support each category. Adding page numbers would allow quick access to a specific entry.

Contents

Title Page
Dimension Chart
Theme and Organization
Section 1: Credentials, Experiences, and Honors
- Resume
- Transcript
- NTE Scores
- Final Evaluation by Supervising Teacher
- List of All Classroom Experiences
- Kappa Delta Pi Reflection and Certificate

Section 2: Philosophy of Education and Professional Development Plan
- My Philosophy of Education
- Professional Development Plan
- Professional Development Plan Reflection
- Comments on Professional Development Plan by Supervising Teacher
- Proactive Behavior Strategies
- Reflection on Behavior Management Articles and Text
- Professional Development Experiences

Section 3: Lessons and Activities
- "Moondance" Lesson
- Example of Student's Work
- Evaluation of Lesson by University Supervisor
- *Word Problems with Regrouping* Lesson
- Self-Evaluation
- Evaluation by Supervising Teacher
- Personal Response Binders
- Math Diagnostics
- Math Adaptations

Section 4: Unit Plan: Exploring Forces
- Unit Plan Overview
- Day-by-Day Activities (including three lesson plans, samples of student's work, self-evaluations, peer evaluation, evaluation by supervising teacher, and evaluation by college supervisor)
- Supplementary Activities

Source: Professional Portfolio of Emily Anne Cosden

This is an example of an electronic portfolio home page. The home page should include a brief introduction to your portfolio and a navigation system. The links in the table of contents allow the reviewer to quickly access the documents in each area. If the portfolio reviewer wanted to learn about your classroom management, he or she would click the Classroom Management link, which would then take them to a menu of categories related to your classroom management artifacts. This example illustrates what the reviewer might see if he or she clicked on the category of seating arrangement.

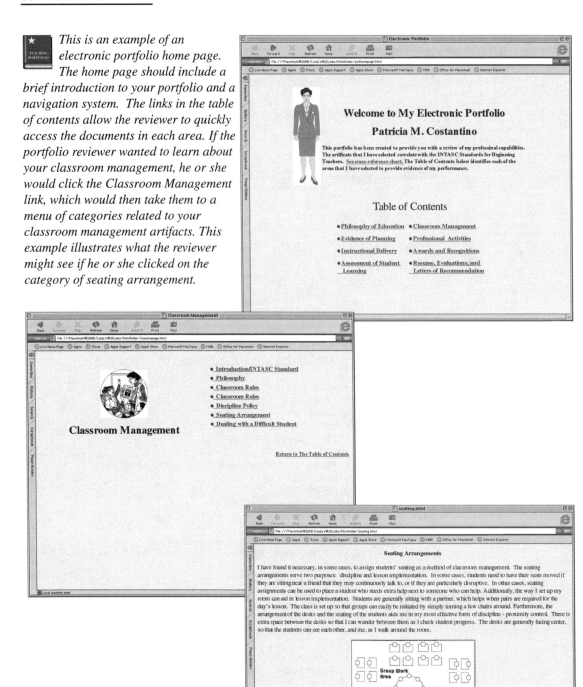

Source: Professional Portfolio of Rosanna Calabrese

Patchwork Portfolio of Rosanna Calabrese

> TANYA LOVED LISTENING TO HER GRANDMOTHER TALK ABOUT THE PATCHWORK QUILT AS SHE CUT AND STITCHED TOGETHER THE SCRAPS OF COLORFUL FABRIC. A SCRAP OF BLUE FROM BROTHER JIM'S FAVORITE OLD PANTS, A PIECE OF GOLD LEFT OVER FROM TANYA'S CHRISTMAS DRESS, A BRIGHT SQUARE FROM TANYA'S HALLOWEEN COSTUME—ALL FIT TOGETHER TO MAKE A QUILT OF MEMORIES.
>
> from The Patchwork Quilt
> Valerie Floundry

As individual scraps of fabric in a patchwork quilt tell a unique story and come together to create a unified work of art, it is my hope that the individual patches of this portfolio tell the story of my professional development and achievement as a teacher candidate. This document is truly my quilt of memories.

This set of artifacts introduces a portfolio developed around the theme of Patchwork Quilts. It includes an introductory narrative and graphic linking performance standards with the theme. These introductory artifacts provide a rationale for the organization and thematic framework of the portfolio.

Source: Professional Portfolio of Rosanna Calabrese

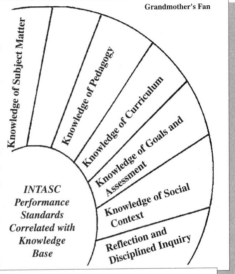

Grandmother's Fan

- Knowledge of Subject Matter
- Knowledge of Pedagogy
- Knowledge of Curriculum
- Knowledge of Goals and Assessment
- Knowledge of Social Context
- Reflection and Disciplined Inquiry

INTASC Performance Standards Correlated with Knowledge Base

Quilts

It is a pleasure to share this professional portfolio with you. It is my hope that the pages genuinely document my achievement of the standards established for teacher candidates.

The theme of this professional portfolio is "quilts." Quilts are works of art that are created to tell stories or document life experiences. Each patch is special and has been designed for a special purpose or inspiration. Together the patches create a unified work of art that tell an even greater story. I believe that education mirrors these qualities of a quilt. Education is a multifaceted discipline that is made up of very special methods of inquiry, ways of knowing, and pedological strategies. Each classroom is a unique community comprised of individual learners with their own fears, interests, talents, and abilities. Education and the classroom are unique quilts that tell the story of our society's present and fosters its future.

I have chosen the College of Education standards for teacher candidates as the organizational framework for this portfolio. These standards are a compilation of expectations of graduates of the College of Education as well as the Interstate New Teacher Assessment and Support Consortium (INTASC) Principles. INTASC standards articulate various beliefs, dispositions, and performances teacher candidates should possess. I believe that through my education, as well as experience in the classroom, I have achieved those standards.

In order to present a theme that is genuine and valid, I spent a great deal of time researching the history and various attributes of quilts. Each section, which is a series of documents demonstrating my achievement of the INTASC standards, begins with a web of attributes of the respective standard. The designs of the graphic organizers are actual traditional quilt patches. The names of the design are under the patches.

This portfolio is a work in progress, as I continue to develop with each experience and reflection. It may never be finished, as I feel I will never be completely developed. It would be a shame to declare myself educated at the conference of my undergraduate degree. Bishop Crieghton once said, "The true objective of education is to leave a man continually asking questions." I have not asked all my questions yet, and I hope I never cease exploring and learning.

Source: Professional Portfolio of Rosanna Calabrese

Introduction

This professional portfolio is designed to give the viewer a small glimpse into the type of professional educator I am both in and out of the classroom. In this portfolio I have included many examples of my personal and professional work. The reader will find that adolescent development is the focus of my teaching. Inside I have attempted to highlight aspects of my professional development while keeping in mind my first priority—the academic and social development of young adults.

Becoming a professional teacher will enable me to not only impart my knowledge of the social studies to my students but also to help mold and construct successful citizens and members of our society. I will strive t[...] active members of the [...] country. Students n[...] instructors in all that l[...] become one of a num[...] for all my students.

Source: Professional Portfolio of Scott Mooney

Portfolio introductions may also be narratives, without graphics, explaining the focus of the portfolio and the teacher's philosophy of education. If narratives are used, they should be no longer than one page. Narrative entries that are lengthy may not be read by the reviewer.

Philosophy of Education

Society pulls students in many different directions. Children have been taught to spend more time watching television than working on schoolwork. Subsequently, teachers have been forced to design activities that constantly re-engage their students. I feel that it is the teacher's job to provide an enriching environment in which the student can grow mentally and academically. This environment must attempt to counteract the media-generated negativity that is constantly battering our young students.

Students learn in numerous unique ways. The teacher should provide varying classroom activities to allow for each of these students to showcase his or her own distinctive method of learning. Students in my classroom will be empowered to achieve, as well as receive motivation to take risks and responsibility for their own education.

Choices should be made available for the student to actively participate in the learning process. Teachers should feel support in trying new ideas and finding new ways to stimulate and propagate academic growth. We as teachers should assume that students can and will achieve to their highest level. We should take the stance that we do not know all, and that we are merely resources to the student along their larger educational journey.

Source: Professional Portfolio of Scott Mooney

Philosophy of Education

My philosophy of education is perpetually evolving. Whether I am a novice or a master at my craft, I will always be a learner and a teacher. Each day I learn from my students, my school, and my community. I then transform these lessons into knowledge that I can use to better understand and help my students, to better serve my school, and to better contribute to my community. Although I cannot definitively state my philosophy of education in a short, concise paragraph, there are four major components that guide my thinking as an educator.

Individual Learner's Needs -- All students can learn; however, it cannot be assumed that they learn in the same ways. In order to meet the needs and concerns of each student, a variety of approaches is necessary to address all learning styles, levels of ability, and levels of motivation.

Student Empowerment -- Students will be motivated to learn if they are given democratic control of their learning. When students are given choices regarding the framework of content material, structure of the class, and classroom policies and procedures, they will take ownership in the process that is rightfully theirs.

Classroom and School as a Community -- School is more than a place to receive an academic education. It is important that students feel as if they belong so that they can form real, lasting social connections. To achieve this goal, students, staff, and parents must get involved in activities and work together, as a team, inside and outside of the classroom to build community.

Teacher as a Lifelong Learner -- Le
a lifelong process. This process req
commitment to learn more in the content are
educational research and strategies, and ong

Realizing that there are differences a
whether it be in culture, learning ability,
education, in my classroom, will unite differ
attained by a cooperative effort from everyo
be understood and before my students ca
question, and reflect for themselves, I must
as they must understand each other. With t
in mind, I enthusiastically welcome the cha
a positive impression on the lives of student

Source: Professional Portfolio of Rosanna Calabrese

This set of items illustrates two ways of representing a philosophy of education. The example on the left begins with a general introduction to the philosophy then highlights four major components of the philosophy. The final paragraph provides a short conclusion.

This graphic organizer links various elements of a teacher's philosophy of education. It can be shown during an interview when the question, "What is your philosophy of education?" is asked. It allows you to have a visual reminder of the important attributes of your philosophy.

Philosophy of Education

resources parents staff development
professional literature and organizations
community assessments

technology books teacher
parents community
self-assessment

utilizes

utilizes

Teacher as Learner — motivates → **Student as Learner**

creates

builds

self-esteem
social skills
thinking skills

Supportive Environment

encourages   constructs   organizes

every student response & participation
risks
multiculturalism
cooperative learning
divergent thinking

meaningful experiences
link to prior knowledge
integrated subjects
challenge equal to support

Knowledge

Source: Professional Portfolio of Lauren T. Costas

Essential Dimensions of Teaching

Throughout my portfolio I mention the Essential Dimensions of Teaching in numerous instances. These dimensions are ten performance-based standards for guiding career-long development that the State of Maryland requires all future-teaching candidates to demonstrate in order to be considered a highly effective educator. The dimensions are as follows:

Teachers Candidates and Teachers Will:

1) Demonstrate mastery of appropriate academic disciplines and a repertoire of teaching techniques.
2) Demonstrate an understanding that knowledge of the learner's physical, cognitive, emotional, social and cultural development is the basis of effective teaching.
3) Incorporate a multicultural perspective which integrates culturally diverse resources, including those from the learner's family and community.
4) Demonstrate a knowledge of strategies for integrating students with special needs into the regular classroom.
5) Use valid assessment approaches, both formal and informal, which are age-appropriate and address a variety of developmental needs, conceptual abilities, curriculum outcomes and school goals.
6) Organize and manage a classroom using approaches supported by student learning needs, research, best practice, and expert opinion.
7) Use computer and computer-related technology to meet student and professional needs.
8) Demonstrate an understanding that classrooms and schools are sites of ethical, social, and civic activity.
9) Collaborate with the broad educational community, including parents, businesses, and social service agencies.
10) Engage in careful analysis, problem-solving, and reflection in all aspects of teaching.

The small footprint labels in the bottom corners of each page are to help in identifying pieces of my work that demonstrate each of the above dimensions.

Reflections and captions found on both blue and yellow paper (with the mountain symbol) throughout my portfolio are also explanations that identify aspects of my teaching that meet these ten dimensions.

Source: Professional Portfolio of Kate Maczis

These two introductory portfolio entries explain how performance standards and portfolio documentation are related. The entry on the left lists the standards used, and the chart below cross-references each standard with the supporting artifacts. The teacher also included icons on each portfolio document that supported a standard. The icons alerted the reviewer to the connection between the artifact and the standard.

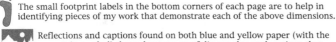

Essential Dimensions of Teaching Portfolio Guide

Artifacts	1	2	3	4	5	6	7	8	9	10
Computer Software							*			
Software Evaluation: Bailey's Bookhouse							*			
Software Integration Project	*			*	*		*			*
Computers and Special Needs: Research Paper				*			*			
Preschool Inventory							*		*	
Daily Assessment Packet				*			*			
Reflections and Interpretations of the Woodcock-Johnson Psycho-education Battery					*		*			
Performance Assessment Task	*				*		*			
Case Study of Caitlin/Parent Conference Materials		*							*	
Case Study of Kevin		*								
Lesson: Reading for a Literary Experience: Who's in the Shed?	*				*		*			*
Lesson: Exploring Three-Letter Words Using Sound Boxes and Letter Tiles						*	*			*
Lesson: The Gingerbread Man: Using Illustrations to Create A Story	*			*	*	*				*
Lesson: Examining Point of View and Story Elements in Fairy Tales: The Three Little Pigs	*				*					*
Lesson: Aquarium Visit Follow-up Activities	*				*		*		*	
Lesson: Insect Memory Game	*			*	*	*	*			*
Literature Assignment	*				*					
Lesson: Jelly Beans for Sale: Understanding the Value of a Quarter	*			*		*	*			
Lesson: Converting Written Time into Digital Time	*			*	*		*			
Lesson: Maps for Parents				*	*	*	*		*	
Theme Development	*	*								
Curriculum Assignment	*	*							*	

Source: Professional Portfolio of Kate Maczis

Theme and Organization

When I began the process of constructing my portfolio, I decided to choose a theme that would reflect my feelings about being an educator. The theme "Committed to a World of Learning" came to me one day as I was driving home from Milbrook. I was sitting in traffic thinking about what I could say that would represent my dedication to the learning process. Throughout my entire life I have enjoyed learning. In my career as a teacher, I hope to pass my love of knowledge on to my students.

The organization of my portfolio is also somewhat deliberate. For example, I chose not to have a multiculturalism section because I believe that multiculturalism should be so ingrained in teaching that it cannot be separated out. Every aspect of teaching (lessons, parent involvement, and related experiences) is permeated by multiculturalism. I also chose not to have a separate section for assessment. Every day in the classroom I assess students' progress. The assessments may be formal or informal, but all are an integral part of teaching. Similarly, I do not have a section about technology. The key focus of technology in education is to integrate the technology so it becomes a part of teaching, just as motivation of manipulatives. The sections that I did choose to create incorporate multiculturalism, assessment, and technology. I created the parent involvement section to highlight and draw attention to the importance of developing relationships with parents. The lesson plans lessons and small group activities that w needs. Finally, the related experiences s have participated in outside of the classr

Source: Professional Portfolio of Emily Anne Cosden

 The introductory entries presented here are two more examples of how to let the portfolio reviewer know your thinking behind the organization of the portfolio documentation. The chart below is a different version of how you can cross-reference performance standards with all the artifacts that relate to the standard.

Dimension 1	Reflection on Behavior Management Articles and Text Professional Development Experiences Lesson: "Moondance" Lesson: "Word Problems with Regrouping" Math Adaptations Unit Plan: Forces Lesson: "In, On, Under, and Through"
Dimension 2	Theme and Organization Philosophy of Education Word of the Month Math Diagnostics Friday Folders and Anecdotal Records Individual Behavior Charts Behavior Certificates
Dimension 3	Theme and Organization Professional Development Exercises Philosophy of Education Personal Response Binders Classroom Reflection Seating Arrangement Word of the Month Lesson: "In, On, Under, and Through" Newsletters
Dimension 4	Theme and Organization Letter from Ms. Prucino, IST teacher Math Adaptations Lesson: "Moondance" Reflection on Special Education Experience Lesson: "In, On, Under, and Through"
Dimension 5	Theme and Organization Philosophy of Education Professional Development Experiences Lesson: "Moondance" Friday Folders and Anecdotal Records Math Diagnostics Informal Literacy Interview Formative and Summative Assessments from Unit Plan: Forces
Dimension 6	Philosophy of Education Proactive Behavior Strategies Reflection on Behavior Management Articles and Text Classroom Meetings Seating Arrangement Individualized Goal Charts Behavior Certificates

Source: Professional Portfolio of Emily Anne Cosden

Professional Goals

Since I began teaching in the fall of 1995, I have set several professional goals for myself. Some of these I have met, others I am working to achieve. My goals are as follows:

- *To enhance my knowledge of technology and integrate its use into daily instruction.*

- *To motivate students to achieve success in academics and extracurricular activities.*

- *To create various performance-based activities for students that reflect MSPAP instruction and the Maryland Learning Outcomes.*

- *To promote reading among all students in order to raise their level of interest and ability.*

- *To develop strategies to assist students with their organizational skills as well as my own.*

- *To pursue a Master's Degree program in technology education.*

This ☺ icon, located on various pages throughout my portfolio, indicates that one of my professional goals has been met to some degree.

Source: Professional Portfolio of Ryan Imbriale

 Including a list of your professional goals provides information to the portfolio reviewer about your future interests and commitment to growth.

Source: Professional Portfolio of Maria Giovanna Marsili

Short- and Long-Term Goals

I have learned a great deal over the past three years of teaching. I have always loved children and have wanted to make a difference in their lives. Thanks to my experience in the classroom, I now know how to make a positive change in children's lives. As an educator, I have set and achieved many goals. My main goals, which are stated on my Professional Development Plan (PDP), were to explore ways to adapt my lessons to meet the individual needs of my students, to implement multicultural activities, and to maintain effective classroom management. I am very fortunate that I set these goals because they helped me stay focused on becoming a more effective educator.

I feel as if I set realistic short- and long-term goals for myself. My short-term goals included establishing a good rapport with my students, establishing classroom management, and learning techniques and strategies from the experienced teachers I worked with. My long-term goals were to become a more effective educator, to make my students feel comfortable and excited about learning, and to truly know how it feels to be a classroom teacher. I feel as if my internship has given me the opportunity to achieve my goals.

As a part of my one-year intensive internship, I was expected to observe other teachers. I decided to observe a first-year fourth-grade teacher, the music teacher, a third-grade teacher, and a fifth-grade teacher. I greatly enjoyed these experiences. I learned how other teachers interact with their students, various management techniques, and what students are held accountable for in other grades. I was especially grateful for the time I spent with the music teacher. It is not very often that classroom teachers have the time to visit special area classrooms. This was a very enlightening and interesting experience.

I definitely plan on establishing short- and long-term goals for my first year of teaching. Some of my goals for my first year of teaching will remain the same. As I am faced with a new group of students, I will need to establish a good rapport and classroom management techniques that will work for those students. One short-term goal I want to work on is incorporating the reading stances into my lessons. I feel this is very important and I did not have much practice doing so in my internship. I always intend on pursuing my goal of becoming a more effective educator. I think when teachers lose sight of this goal, their students suffer. I want my students to have the

 Professional goals may also be effectively communicated in a narrative form or chart. Many teachers often use both a narrative introduction and an accompanying chart. The chart below shows how a teacher's professional development plan relates to the INTASC standards.

Professional Development Plan

INTASC Performance Standards	Action Plan	Implementation
The Learner The teacher candidate stimulates student reflection on prior knowledge and links new ideas to already familiar ideas, making connections to students' experiences, providing opportunities for active engagement, manipulation, and testing of ideas and materials, and encouraging Students to assume responsibility. The teacher candidate assesses individual Differences, and designs and delivers Instruction appropriate to students' stages of development, cultural backgrounds, Learning styles, strengths, and needs.	1. What do the students already know (and have done) about the topics I will teach? 2. How can I get the children interested in activities and stimulate them to learn? 3. How do I adapt my lessons to work for the different learning levels represented in my classroom?	1. I will review what the students have already done with my mentor teacher before teaching a lesson and I will activate the students' prior knowledge by asking review questions at the beginning of a lesson. 2. I will implement child-centered activities in a manner that excite children. Examples of this are the patterning activities I have done and the measurement activities I will implement in the future. 3. I will make appropriate adjustments, including using different manipulatives for different groups.
Goals & Assessment The teacher candidate uses a variety of formal and informal assessment techniques to enhance his or her knowledge of learners, evaluate student's progress and performances, and modify teaching and learning strategies.	1. What kinds of formal and informal assessments are done in kindergarten?	1. I will take part in observing and administering some formal assessments that are used, including Title I assessments and ISM assessments. I will also discuss with my mentor teacher how the many informal assessments, such as observations, collection of homework, and questions are used in kindergarten.
Subject Matter The teacher candidate evaluates teaching resources and curriculum materials for their comprehensiveness, accuracy, and usefulness for representing particular ideas and concepts.	1. What curriculum objectives are children in kindergarten expected to pass? 2. How can I makeup lessons to cover multiple objectives accurately?	1. I have looked at some curriculum guides already and plan to study more over the next few weeks. 2. I have made up some lessons that cover one main objective, but within these lessons, the student think critically, explore and use multiple skills to draw conclusion to their thinking.

Source: Professional Portfolio of Denise Logsdon

Source: Professional Portfolio of Rosanna Calabrese

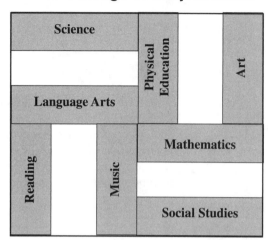

Knowledge of Subject Matter

Roman Square Patch

Knowledge of Subject Matter

Science

Physical Education

Art

Language Arts

Reading

Music

Mathematics

Social Studies

These examples are introductions to a portfolio section that documents a teacher's knowledge of subject matter. They are part of the portfolio that is based on the theme of Patchwork Quilts. Included is the specific standard being documented, a philosophy statement, an explanation of how the teacher's goal was achieved, and a listing of portfolio entries that support the teacher's knowledge and practice toward the achievement of this standard.

Standard: The teacher candidate understands the central concepts, assump...
are cen...
knowle...
c) Scie...

As each scrap of fabric in a patchwork quilt tells a unique story and comes together to create a unified work of art...

...it is my belief that individual disciplines possess unique characteristics. Because education is a profession that employs its own methods of inquiry, research, and pedagogical strategies, each discipline area—Language Arts, Math, Science, Social Studies, and Fine Arts—has its own methods. I believe that in order to present students with learning experiences that are authentic, meaningful, and demonstrating the interconnectedness of knowledge and skills, it is imperative to be articulate in the distinct dimensions of each area. This involves knowing and practicing the various methods of inquiry and developmental theories within each discipline.

I have attended to this goal by actively researching current perspectives and ways of knowing within each disciplinary area. As a result of my knowledge of subject matter, I have been able to define the objectives within each discipline, as well as set developmentally appropriate goals for my students. I use this knowledge to design and develop integrated thematic units that elicit a variety of student engagement and use of thinking skills. When students are participating in learning activities that combine these skills and ways of knowing, they are able to see the unified work of art, the integration of knowledge and skills. I have chosen the following artifacts to document my knowledge and active practice of subject matter knowledge in the classroom:

- **Dienes' Levels of Mathematical Learning**—This entry demonstrates my knowledge of different stages of mathematical learning. I used this model to design and develop a unit on fractions.
- **Poyla's Four Steps to Problem Solve**—By articulating the skills and strategies available to problem solve, I am able to expose my students to a fundamental dimension of applied mathematics.
- **Language Arts**—I created this web to graphically organize an author illustrator study on Maurice Sendak. I have illustrated the several dimensions of Language Arts and the methods in which I employed them in a thematic unit.
- **Reading**—This graphic organizer illustrates the three main goals I have for readers in my classroom community and the actions I take to attend to these goals. I believe that these goals allow me to focus my planning and include all dimensions of subject matter.
- **Hands On Science**—This page reflects a general approach I take to provide contexts for science inquiry in my classroom. When purposes and goals of subject matter inquiry are clearly stated, students are empowered to make their own focused investigations.
- **Technology**—Technology plays an active role across all subject matter areas in my classroom. Technology has become a new form of functional literacy and has its own distinct qualities.

Source: Professional Portfolio of Rosanna Calabrese

Evidence of Planning

Planning is the first step toward creating a quality atmosphere in the classroom. I have been witness to many teachers who have suffered from a lack of planning, and their classroom environment became the unfortunate casualty of that lack of foresight. The reader will see that I have the skills necessary to create a structured environment in which the primary responsibility of the student is to become a successful learner. Unit, weekly, and daily lesson plans are the first step in the creation of a quality environment. These plans allow the teacher to become more familiar with the material as well as initiate a thought process that will lead to more detailed investigation into the subject matter.

I have also included numerous examples of activities I designed and implemented in the classroom. I do not rely solely on the planning of curriculum guides in my teaching and feel more than comfortable designing thought-provoking activities for classroom use. These activities are goal oriented with state and national objectives kept in minds at all times. The use of political cartoons, letters of complaint with their appropriate scoring rubric, and a check-writing project are illustrated. Also included are examples of both formative an

The two narratives shown here are section introductions to the planning and instructional delivery categories of the portfolio. They provide the portfolio reviewer with a short philosophy and rationale for including the selected artifacts.

Source: Professional Portfolio of Scott Mooney

Instructional Delivery

The successful teacher will be able to vary instruction in a number of different ways to accommodate as many students as possible. In a setting full of different nationalities, socioeconomic backgrounds, and races a teacher who can find methods to reach all groups is priceless. This environment forces educators to provide instruction that varies not only day to day but intra-class period also. Teaching block classes allows the instructor to vary instruction far more than does a shorter class period. I have found that it is easier to reach more students in the block-scheduled school due to the longer period of time in class that you have to observe cognition and comprehension.

The reader will find included in this section a number of examples of varying instructional delivery methods. From didactic teaching to cooperative learning methods, structured individual work time to working with small groups, I have attempted to place as many styles as possible into my repertoire. Students deserve to have the most advantageous environment in which to comprehend information. I attempt to provide as much scaffolding as possible, without actually providing answers, during difficult topics. My use of graphic organizers is illustrated as one method that I employ to help students grasp abstract or complex material. Another method I use to aid students' under-standing is through the use of computers in class. I believe that making a student more comfortable with technology, and then using that technology to assist in the teaching process, will alleviate some of the pressure placed on the student. Creating a comfortable environment and providing the proper tools to succeed are essential to each other and to the learning process.

Source: Professional Portfolio of Scott Mooney

Source: Professional Portfolio of Lauren T. Costas

Knowledge of Pedagogy

The teacher candidate understands a variety of instructional models (general, discipline specific, and behavioral), the principles of effective classroom management, human motivation and behavior, and has a knowledge of the interpersonal skills that promote positive working relationships with all students and adults in the educational community.

Contents:

I. Introduction
II. Experiences
III. Documents
   1. The "B" Wheel and Instructional Strategies
   2. The "M" Wheel and Motivation and Management Strategies

The sample entries shown here provide the introduction to a section of the portfolio that documents performance in the area of pedagogy. This set of items includes a statement of the performance standard with a list of the contents included in this section, an introductory narrative about pedagogy, and a list of experiences related to this teacher's accomplishments in the area of pedagogy.

Introduction

I believe that students will be motivated to learn in a supportive environment in which they have a sense of ... Students should be motivated to learn ... as well as become responsible for the positive ... consequences of their behavior. The teacher ... de students in the creation of class rules and ... ruction that is developmentally appropriate, ... and engaging is the best form of classroom ... . In this environment, the teacher uses a balance ... humor, consistency in holding students ... for their behaviors, and fairness to accomplish ...

... ally, I am always working to improve upon that ... ave tried and implemented many classroom ... t strategies throughout my student teaching ... I believe it is important to be flexible and to ... tegies. These strategies are evident throughout ... ts in this portfolio. For that reason, this section ...

... ection is structured into two sections: ... al strategies and motivation/management ... believe that the two work together to create a ... classroom climate. My management and ... philosophies are in sync with the two following ... anizers that I was introduced to early in my ... program. I believe they best

Source: Professional Portfolio of Lauren T. Costas

Experiences with Pedagogy

Created units of instruction following logical scope and sequence patterns.

Developed lesson plans following a motivational format: starting with an anticipatory set, followed by guided practice, independent work, and a closure.

Used cooperative learning strategies to promote proactive group work: T-charts, modeled Think-Pair-Share, assigned roles to all group members (recorder, reporter, time keeper...).

Incorporated Every Student Response techniques into whole group activities by using hand signals, manipulatives, writing, etc.

Engaged students by weaving prior knowledge, literature, hands-on activities, sense of humor, and students' interests into lesson plans.

Used many classroom management strategies, both intrinsic and extrinsic, to remain flexible in varying situations (clapping, lights, individualized programs, contracts, table stars, chance tickets, eating lunch with teacher, extra computer time, etc.).

Source: Professional Portfolio of Lauren T. Costas

Examples of Instructional Artifacts

As you select materials that illustrate your teaching effectiveness, it is important to include a variety of artifacts. However, it will be more meaningful for the portfolio reviewer to see a set of items that are related to the context and sequence of instruction. The first seven examples focus on portfolio documents that represent the context and sequence of an instructional unit. The remaining examples are not necessarily connected in this fashion, but provide ideas for a variety of ways to present your work.

INTRODUCTION

The following document represents four weeks of instruction with thirty-three students from diverse cultural backgrounds. I selected this unit because . . . I modified the unit because . . . I modified the level of difficulty to meet student needs by . . . I intentionally designed lessons to motivate students by . . . I planned collaboratively with other teachers . . .

PERSONAL REFLECTION

As a result of teaching this unit, I realized/gained insight about:

- timing of lessons

- choice of materials

- students' social skills

- choice of assessment tools

Changes I will make in future instruction are . . .

The example on the left is intended to provide you with ideas for what to include in an introduction and reflection when presenting several related artifacts. Your introductions and reflections will be unique to your unit and personal goals.

Introductory Items

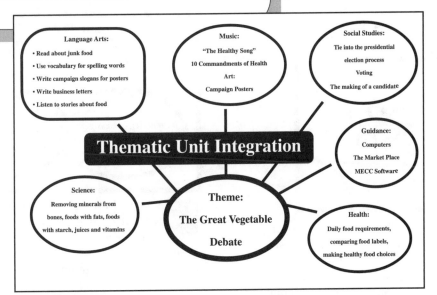

Source: *Professional Portfolio of Lisa Wehausen*

 This graphic organizer allows the portfolio reviewer to see your interdisciplinary approach to instruction at a glance.

Planning

Including a unit outline and one sample of your best lesson provides the portfolio reviewer with a sense of the entire unit of instruction as well as a more detailed description of your individual lesson.

UNIT OVERVIEW

I. Objectives

II. Teaching Learning Activities

III. Evaluating Learning Activities

IV. Culminating Activity

LESSON PLAN

- Objective
- Anticipatory Set
- Instructional input
- Modeling
- Check for Understanding
- Guided Practice
- Independent Practice
- Closure

COOPERATIVE LEARNING
PEER TEACHING
CONFERENCING
WORKING IN PAIRS
HANDS-ON

INCLUSION
MULTICULTURALISM

CONCEPT ATTAINMENT

REFLECTION

INSTRUCTIONAL STRATEGIES

ROLE PLAYING

GRAPHIC ORGANIZERS
WEBBING

INTERDISCIPLINARY
CONNECTIONS

WHOLE CLASS INSTRUCTION
EVERY STUDENT RESPONSE
THINK-PAIR-SHARE

Instructional Delivery

You can create a graphic organizer similar to the example on the left to highlight all the instructional strategies used during this unit.

Assessment

Teacher Developed Performance Assessments

Student Self-Assessments and Work Samples

Written Notes on Observations of Students' Progress

Most units of instruction have a culminating activity. If you have implemented a special project or event to bring together all the learning that has occurred, include a photograph or narrative about this activity

Student learning is the most important outcome of your instruction. You will need to provide evidence of your student's achievement resulting from your instruction. Include samples of assessments and the results of student learning.

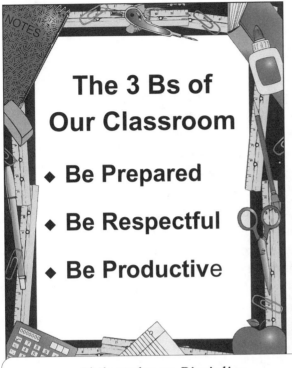

The 3 Bs of Our Classroom

- ◆ **Be Prepared**
- ◆ **Be Respectful**
- ◆ **Be Productive**

CREATING A POSITIVE CLIMATE IN MY ART ROOM

The establishment of a positive and productive classroom environment is, aside from the quality of teaching, the most important function of a teacher. Without a healthy and enjoyable learning environment, it is impossible for students and teachers to reach their full educational potentials.

I believe that the best way to create an effective classroom climate is for the teacher to recognize and accommodate the physical and emotional needs of the students, interests and motivation, individual learning styles, ability levels, and the development of interpersonal communication skills through group involvement. It is my goal for this environment to be as aesthetically pleasing as it is functional. To accomplish this, I will employ the use of visual aids of various art and life objects, student works, sculpture and models, good lighting, and even occasional soft music to promote better concentration.

interesting and nurturing classroom character ...nbined with effective teaching strategies and style ...l provide students, and teachers alike, with an ...oyable and rewarding educational experience that ...l provide a foundation for learning based on ...piness and success.

Source: Professional Portfolio of Mat DeMunbrun

Philosophy on Discipline

I expect all students to show both their classmates and me proper respect at all times. By using a variety of methods to ensure that the students work as a team, I attempt to foster a feeling of togetherness and responsibility for one another in the students. Working in groups during class, using proper names when referring to classmates, participating in group projects, and participating in community activities as a class are just a few of the methods I will employ to ensure that the class works together. I believe that if the students feel that their success depends on their classmates, and their classmates' success depends on them, they will work wholeheartedly toward a mutual goal. Along with the components of motivation that I have listed on the following page, I will take the following steps in resolving conflict:

- Wait Time
- Proximity Control
- Informal Conference with Student
- Formal Conference with Student
- Personal Performance Contract
- Extra Involvement in Academic Setting
- After School Detention if Applicable
- Parental Contact
- Guidance Contact
- Parent/Teacher Conference
- Administrative Contact
- Formal Referral

I work very hard to develop and maintain a working relationship with every student. I will never rest if a student requests assistance or guidance. I will also attempt to carry a student only so far. Students, as young adults, need to realize that they are increasingly responsible for their own actions, consequently, they will need to meet me halfway. My relationship with students is based on their attitude alone. I never use other's opinions to develop my own. A relationship is a two-way street and I expect truth and commitment to that relationship.

Source: Professional Portfolio of Scott Mooney

The portfolio documents shown here and on the following page provide examples of different entries related to managing and organizing the classroom. Artifacts explaining your classroom rules, room arrangement, strategies for discipline, and your approach to creating a positive classroom climate reveals valuable information that provides insight to the portfolio reviewer about your potential to effectively manage the classroom.

Seating Arrangements

I have found it necessary, in some cases, to assign students' seating as a method of classroom management. The seating arrangements serve two purposes: discipline and lesson implementation. In some cases, students need to have their seats moved if they are sitting near a friend whom they may continuously talk to, or if they are particularly disruptive. In other cases, seating assignments can be used to place a student who needs extra help next to someone who can help. Additionally, the way I set up my room can aid in lesson implementation. Students are generally sitting with a partner, which helps when pairs are required for the day's lesson. The class is set up so that groups can easily be initiated by simply turning a few chairs around. Furthermore, the arrangement of the desks and the seating of the students aids me in my most effective form of discipline—proximity control. There is extra space between the desks so that I can wander between them as I check student progress. The desks are generally facing center so that the students can see e

Group Work
Area

Lesson Presentation Area

Chart Stand

Chalk Board

A narrative description discussing your rationale for organizing the classroom allows the portfolio reviewer to understand your thinking and decision making about the arrangement of the classroom. A seating chart provides a visual that correlates with the written explanation.

Reflection on Behavior Management Articles and Text

Several weeks into the semester, my cooperating teacher gave me the article, "Some First Steps for Improving Classroom Discipline," and the text, *Teaching Children to Care: Management in the Responsive Classroom.* She recommended that I read the article and selected chapters from the text that were beneficial to her during her first year of teaching. Both texts highlight behavior strategies that can be used in the classroom to maintain a positive environment. After reading the selections, she and I sat down and discussed what I had read. We brainstormed times when we used the techniques in the classroom and reflected on their success or failure. The following chart outlines the behavior strategies that I have used in the classroom and how effective they were for me.

Source: Professional Portfolio of Emily Anne Cosden

Strategy	Source	Description	Reflection on Effectiveness
No Means No	"Some First Steps For Improving Classroom Discipline" by David Hopkins	Say what you mean and mean what you say.	Highly effective with all students in the class. Students react positively when expectations are established and constant.
Limit Setting	"Some First Steps for Improving Classroom Discipline" by David Hopkins	Relax Move slowly Turn, look, wait Prompt (hand, verbal, or eye)	Highly effective with some students, moderately effective with others. Some students respond with exaggerated back talk.
Dealing with Back talk	"Some First Steps for Improving Classroom Discipline" by David Hopkins	Types of Behaviors: •Helplessness •Denial •Blaming •Accusing teacher of professional incompetence Action: Provide opportunities for positive attention getting.	Highly effective with all students. Verbally responding to any form of back talk reinforces it with the student. Many students who need attention get it negatively through back talk.
Self-Controls	*Teaching Children to Care: Management in the Responsive Classroom* by Ruth Sidney Charney	Give students the power to make decisions after modeling effective self-control.	Highly effective with most students, but must be done from first day of school. Beginning self-control training during the year is very difficult.
Appropriate Comments	*Teaching Children to Care: Management In the Responsive Classroom* by Ruth Charney	Specific (name a behavior or accomplishment Positive ("Show me what you will do" not "Don't do that") Comments must be encouraging (they support children's efforts).	Highly effective with all students. Many students have had experiences of frequently being told "no" or "stop." This strategy redirects a specific behavior in a way that does not embarrass or hurt the child.

Source: Professional Portfolio of Emily Anne Cosden

Evidence that supports your commitment to learn more and improve your classroom management provides the portfolio reviewer with additional information about you as a professional teacher. This entry is an example of implementing various behavior management strategies and reflecting on the effectiveness of each strategy.

WEEKLY LESSON PLANS			
History - Colonies	Mods 1,2,3,5,6		Mrs. Imbriale

10/14
SWBAT:
differentiate between indentured servitude and slavery.
	Warm-Up =
	List the types of farming practiced in the following colonial regions:
	① New England
	② Middle
	③ Southern
		I. Review Outline Map
		II. Definition
		  A. indentured servant
		  B. slave
		III. Primary Source Document - I.S.
			Homework =
			None!

10/15 SWBAT: compare the lives of an indentured servant and a slave using primary source documents	What is the primary difference between an indentured servant and a slave?	I. Review I.S. Primary Source II. Read slave document III. Complete Venn diagram	Homework = Current Events Abstract
10/16 SWBAT: _investigate_ the conditions of the Middle Passage by analyzing a graphic.	List 10 words that you feel would best describe the conditions on a slave ship.	I. Review differences from yesterday II. Analyze the graphic of the slave ship - answer quest. III. Brief discussion	Homework = Vocabulary ① slavery ② indentured servant ③ middle passage ④ witchcraft * ⑤ brochure *
10/17 SWBAT: express their feelings regarding slavery by composing an essay	Identify the name given to the journey from Africa	I. Pre-Writing II. Rough Dr III. Peer Edit	Homework = "Think Ab
10/18 SWBAT: illustrate an African-American slave tale.	Why do people tell stories?	(Explain im of oral stor II. Illustrat III. Write br caption	

Weekly Plann

Source: Professional Portfolio of Merritt Imbriale

Daily Planning

Subject __US History__ Unit __Colonies - Slavery__ Topic __African-American Storytelling__

Mod __all__ Date __10/18/96__ Text/Materials Needed __The People Could Fly by Virginia Hamilton, paper, colored pencils__

MSPAP Outcome/Skills __people of nation and world, skills and processes, valuing self and others; Soc St/Language Usage/Reading/Writing__

Focusing Students Attention/Warm-Up __Why do people tell stories?__

Statement of Objective Students will be able to: __illustrate an African-American slave tale.__

Introductory/Developmental Activities __Display riddle on the board (p. 159) Telling riddles was second to Briefly discuss importance__

Guided Practice Activities __Have a aloud. ("Carrying the Running-Aways) Students should follow along with their own copy of the story.__

Independent Activities/Meaningful-Use Tasks __Draw an illustration of the story we read. Be sure to label your picture. Then, write a 2 sentence caption for your picture. Be creative; use color.__

Assessment Activities __Students will be assessed on the picture drawn (labels, creativity, etc.) and the caption.__

Closure Activity __Ask 2-3 students to share their pictures. Then, read aloud another riddle to enforce storytelling and the message.__

Homework __Complete illustration, if necessary. Have a great weekend! Reminder: Technology papers/projects due 10/24!__

Source: Professional Portfolio of Merritt Imbriale

Many working portfolios include authentic evidence of planning. By providing an example of your weekly plan with the example of a more detailed daily lesson plan, you are demonstrating your skills in long- and short-term instructional planning.

Source: Professional Portfolio of Rosanna Calabrese

Joana   Samuel   Charles

Sean   Hieu

Miss
Calabrese

These flags represent the diversity of students within
my classroom community. Each flag was selected
because it symbolizes the heritage of at least one
student. Although each flag symbolizes a unique
culture and belief system, together they create a
classroom of students rich with life experiences,
multi-perspectives, and special talents. International
Night is one event designed to share this diversity. In
my classroom, this diversity celebrated every day,

Ma

John

Roberto   Ju

*Examples of activities and
projects that show how you
created a multicultural
perspective in your classroom are
important.*

Incorporating Multiculturalism by Celebrating Woman's History Month

Multiculturalism should be woven through all curriculum via multiple forms. Here is
one way I addressed multiculturalism in my classroom.

Above, you'll see a sample of books I used to integrate multicultural literature and
information into the creation of our Woman's History Quilt. These books tell stories of
women in many cultures: Hispanic, African American, Amish, etc. I enjoy books because
they illustrate similarities among differing cultures. They were used to provide students
with information and motivation for creating a quilt.

This is the quilt
we created to
celebrate famous
women in
history.

Each student created a
square based on the
woman he or she
studied. Students
researched women by
reading and
highlighting
expository text. Some
women we studied
were Harriet Tubman,
Helen Keller, and
Susan B, Anthony etc.

Source: Professional Portfolio of Lauren T. Costas

Source: Professional Portfolio of Ryan Imbriale

Create Your Own Culture
Assignment Sheet

Project Description:
For the next few class periods, you and your "self-chosen" team (maximum 4 persons) will create your own culture. The goal for this project is (1) to introduce you to the sociological term "culture," (2) to enable you to demonstrate your understanding of different cultural attributes, and (3) to be creative while having fun. The project will concentrate on six main areas of sociology and culture. Each member of your team will be responsible for equal contributions to the project. Decide among yourselves who will be responsible for what areas. When you turn in your project, each member must submit a complete Rubric with an evaluation of your group's work as well as a self-evaluation of your contribution.

Written Components: In well-written, complete sentence paragraphs, write a description for each area of your created culture. The details of your culture should be created and discussed with your team members. Each member is responsible for writing up at least one component. The areas within your culture must include the following:
The Name of Your Culture: Be creative (but not silly)!
Family: Determine what the average family is like in the culture you created. Consider such possible areas as family size, income, divorce rate, social status, population, extended or n[...]
what type of ceremonies th[...]

Political Systems: Determ[...]
Consider such possible are[...]
of the people in the govern[...]
and the government, how t[...]
might deal with problems [...]
how are leaders determine[...]
Economy: Determine the[...]
areas as main products, ho[...]
income is, is the economy [...]
export, and is it an industri[...]
Education: Consider poss[...]
of people in schools, the ty[...]
all the people, are there hig[...]
most schooling done by te[...]
they learn.

This double entry is a detailed explanation of a multicultural project with a tool for assessing this assignment. The photographs, not shown here, bring to life student involvement and project outcomes.

Create Your Own Culture
~Rubric~

Written Components:		Student	Teacher
The Name of Your Culture	2 pts.	_____	_____
Family	8 pts.	_____	_____
Political Systems	8 pts.	_____	_____
Economy	8 pts.	_____	_____
Education	8 pts.	_____	_____
Religion	8 pts.	_____	_____
Natural Features	8 pts.	_____	_____
Social Characteristics	8 pts.	_____	_____
Visual Component:	6 pts.	_____	_____
2-3 minute Presentation:	5 pts.	_____	_____
Individual Effort:	5 pts.	_____	_____
Team Efforts:	5 pts.	_____	_____
TOTAL POINTS	**75 pts.**	_____	_____

Student's Comments
(Use back if necessary.)

Teacher's Comments
(Use back if necessary.)

I taught Sociology to eleventh and twelfth graders. This is an example of a project students did to study the components of culture.

Source: Professional Portfolio of Ryan Imbriale

 **SOCIAL CONTEXT**

As each scrap of fabric in a patchwork quilt tells a unique story and comes together to create a unified work...

 These entries illustrate how a teacher bridges home, school, and community experiences to make learning more meaningful for the students.

...the many dimensions of the student's life—home, school, and county—come together to create an educational community. The educational community as a whole permeates almost every aspect of society: families, students, school administrators, economics, politics, culture, etc. The classroom climate and the products of that environment therefore not only affect the students, but society as a whole as well. The individual learners come into the classroom with their own life experiences and values. This classroom community operates in the context of a school community that has its own characteristics, resources, and concerns.

It is my goal as a teacher to use these dimensions as resources to foster authentic, meaningful, and relevant learning experiences. By integrating school and home experiences, as well as demonstrating other community resources, I am able to create student-centered activities that motivate and invite the students to actively participate in their society.

I have chosen the following to documen[t] social experience to support their learning a[...]

- **Montgomery County Recycling Cent[er...]** to be aware and experience the valuabl[...] they live. In order to do that, I research[...] that support the students' classroom le[...]
- **Rumpus Party**—This was a celebrati[on...] our unit on Maurice Sendak. I invite[d...] excited to share their experiences wit[h...] and the families demonstrated their en[...]
- **Newsletter**—This is another method I[...] involved in classroom activities. I solic[...] to reciprocate the sharing of informati[on...]
- **International Night**—This entry de[...] community as well as the appreciation[...] community.
- **Collaboration with Specialists**—In [...] experiences that demonstrate the interc[...] as well as the various ways of knowin[g...] June Cayne, to design a learning activi[ty...] my Maurice Sendak unit.

Source: Professional Portfolio of Rosanna Calabrese

INTEGRATING RECYCLING

The students used Kid Pix to create Earth Day posters. This activity integrated language arts, art, social studies, and technology.

This bulletin board displays student published work. The student wrote books about the many ways an object can be reused instead of thrown in the trash. The titles vary from the <u>Six Lives of a Can</u> to the <u>Ten Lives of a Box.</u>

This is one of the many literature theme baskets I have in the classroom. Students frequently read these to discover more about our subject of inquiry as well as to supplement their learning activities.

Source: Professional Portfolio of Rosanna Calabrese

Didactic Teaching

Although I strive to vary my instru...
possible, it is sometimes necessary...
the students in a more structured...
vidual exploration may allow. Dire...
some cases a limited discussion led...
most efficient method for this disse...
tion. Limiting the use of this meth...
effectiveness. Students who are fo...
after day, to teachers drone on are...
in their own education. This loss...
only to decreased student perform...
management problems also.

Source: Professional Portfolio of Scott Mooney

*These narrative entries
describe two different types
of instructional strategies
with students. Both entries
include a reflection on the
effectiveness of the strategy.*

Cooperative Learning and Jig Saw Teaching
in the Secondary Classroom

Secondary students have the ability to become more familiar with their content through the use of cooperative learning and jig saw teaching. In this example I was interested in the students' becoming familiar with seven examples of slave revolt during the 19th century. Instead of giving the students notes to take and readings for the whole class to complete, I broke the class up into seven different groups based on where they sat in the room. Each group was given a reading on one of the slave revolts and instructed that they would be responsible for teaching the rest of the class the appropriate information to fill in the graphic organizer. I allowed the students to work on their own material for an entire class period (45 minutes) and instructed them that they would be teaching their material at the next class meeting.

Reflection
This activity could have worked even better than it did if the students had participated in something like this previously. I found out that middle school aged students are not skilled in pulling out the truly important material from the text in a manner that allows them to teach the class. I am positive that these students would have been able to master this process after a more structured modeling example and repeated application.

Source: Professional Portfolio of Scott Mooney

Letter of Complaint Project

This assignment will require you to write a letter of complaint to a business. You will choose one of four situations below and write a letter of complaint to someone in authority at that business. This letter is due at the end of class.

The situations are:

1.)   You brought your car into the dealer where you bought it because it was making a funny noise. You are not a car expert so you did not know what was wrong. As you are talking to the service guy, you are getting more and more worried. He spent a half-hour telling you what may be wrong and how it could result in more and more damage to your car. Because you have no experience in fixing cars you are taking his word for it. You leave the car with him and give him permission to fix your car.

   You go to work and at the end of the day you pick up your car. The cashier gives you the bill for $600 and you are very shocked that a small noise could be so costly. You look for someone to explain to you why it is so much but everyone but the cashier is gone for the day. You are told that if you don't pay for the car then you cannot take it home. You need the car for work the next day so you decide to pay the bill and find someone to complain to the next day. The next day you find time to call the dealership and talk to the service guy. He gave you a very technical explanation that you really didn't understand and he seems incapable or unwilling to explain it so that you can understand. You finally hang up the phone thoroughly confused, more than a little angry, and out $600!

2.)   You are shopping for clothes for the next school year. You have a bunch of money that you earned from working over the summer and are ready to spend a lot on a new wardrobe. You know where the good clothes are and you can't wait to buy as much as you can. As you start looking at the clothes for a while, you notice that the service people are ignoring you and running to the older customers to see if they need help. You look around for someone to open a changing room for you to try on some clothes and after 20 minutes, you find someone. That person gives you an attitude that tells you that he or she does not have enough time to spend on you.

   After you have tried on a bunch of clot[...] sales person comes over and looks at w[...] realize that the person is counting the [...] bring them up to the register, you agai[...] to ring your purchases.

Source: Professional Portfolio of Scott Mooney

These two entries provide the portfolio reviewer with artifacts that show how the teacher facilitated thinking and problem solving. The scoring rubric identifies each area of performance expected from the activity.

Student's Name: _____   Date:_____

Letter of Complaint Scoring Rubric

		Your Score	My Score
Format			
•Address in the correct places -	5 pts.	____	____
•Three full paragraphs written -	5 pts.	____	____
•Date and your name in the correct place -	5 pts.	____	____
Content			
Introduction Paragraph			
•Did you explain who you were? -	5 pts.	____	____
•Did you explain what happened to initiate this letter? -			
5 pts.			
Problem Paragraph			
•Did you explain what action the store took?-	5 pts.	____	____
•Did you explain why this action was not satisfactory?-	5 pts.	____	____
Resolution Paragraph			
•Did you explain what you want done?-	5 pts.	____	____
•Did you explain why you thought that this resolution was acceptable or reasonable?-	5 pts.	____	____
Accuracy			
•Did you correctly use one of the situations outlined in the assignment?-	10 pts.	____	____
•Did you address the letter to a reasonable person?	10 pts	____	____
•Did you use words that sounded respectful, full sentences, correct spelling, proper grammar?-	10 pts.	____	____
Total Points	**75 pts.**	____	____

Source: Professional Portfolio of Scott Mooney

Urban, Suburban, and Rural Unit

This unit started with a general overview and introduction to the terms: urban, suburban, and rural. Students were read storybooks that illustrated each type of community and then were asked to search the stories for comparisons and contrasts between the different communities. Graphic Organizers were used to demonstrate their understandings. Each student filled out his or her own diagram. Furthermore, the students wrote poetry, conducted informational interviews, conducted research of a community by examining textbook materials, and created murals.

As a class, we created a visual representation of their individual work. Below is a picture of the beginning of the bulletin board that acted as a constant source of learning during this unit. The students in this picture are working collaboratively to represent the common elements shared by urban, suburban, and rural communities. They brainstormed a variety of residential, recreational, and commercial attributes characteristic of these communities. I wrote their suggestions on cards and the students illustrated the text. When they came back to the floor, students placed the objects on the diagram and explained their reasoning. The students then gave a thumbs up or thumbs down to demonstrate their agreement or disagreement. If a student disagreed, he or she would argue his or her case, and the students together voted on where the card should be placed.

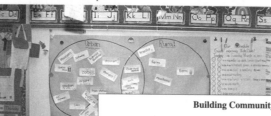

The following documents represent a few
on the big concept of many types of comm
kinds of urban communities. Third, we st
of a suburban community. Lastly, we
communities. Specifically, we stu

Source: Professional Portfolio of Rosanna Calabrese

The entry on the left describes the introductory lesson to a social studies unit. The use of photographs enhance the detailed explanation.

Building Community by Representing a Community

The second grade teachers and student teachers presented their classes with a task. They were asked to fill the following mural paper with their own representation of an Amish community. Creating this mural was an activity set up to promote community building with the classroom, as well as to give the students an opportunity to showcase their new knowledge about one type of rural community.

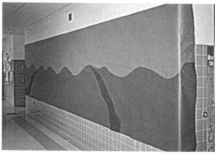

The Final Product

Here is the final product in all its splendor. As you can see, the whole second grade contributed to this colorful representation of an Amish community. The students made all the decisions regarding the mural and were just as proud of their working together as they were of the actual finished product.

Source: Professional Portfolio of Lauren T. Costas

Products such as the before and after mural related to the Urban, Suburban, and Rural Unit illustrate how the students contributed to a group activity.

A Reflection About Journal Writing

Reflecting upon my own education experiences, I remember one teacher who really motivated me and got me excited about learning. He integrated the subject, made science hands-on, and gave us a lot of autonomy. I felt that he appreciated each one of us. One of the methods he used was also one of my favorite, journal writing. The journal writing took place at the beginning and end of every day. We would write anything in the journal from poetry to complaints about the bully on the playground, to jokes or ongoing stories. I really looked forward to that time, especially because I knew that my teacher was going to read it and write something back. He would always write funny or caring comments that valued my perspective and encouraged me to think.

To this day I always valued that teaching strategy. I intend to use it in my own classroom. It offers the students the chance to reflect, release, read, and relate. It also offers the teacher a world of knowledge. It provides the teac̶ daily lives, creativity, sense of hu̶ concerns which can be utilized for l̶ Journals allow students to exp̶ encouraging them to use their wri̶

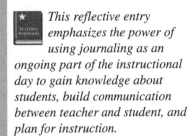

This reflective entry emphasizes the power of using journaling as an ongoing part of the instructional day to gain knowledge about students, build communication between teacher and student, and plan for instruction.

Source: Professional Portfolio of Lauren T. Costas

This entry shows how journals may be used as a method for assessing learning in mathematics.

Journal Assessment

Objective: This method of informal assessment allows me to evaluate individual student comprehension during instruction while reinforcing independent practice.

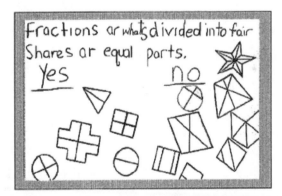

Fractions ar what s divided into fair Shares ar equal parts.
Yes   no

Description: This is a sample from a student's math journal. This entry was an independent practice activity that followed an initiatory concept attainment lesson about fractions. The students used their journals to write the "fraction rule" across their journal pages and to document their analysis of wholes to determine whether they were divided into equal parts. This student's work demonstrates that she has an accurate comprehension of equal parts or fair shares. She is able to discriminate which wholes are fractions and which do not fit the rule. While she was working independently, I asked her a few questions to evaluate her ability to articulate her thought process and defend her judgments. She modeled her thoughts by folding the shapes to demonstrate the equivalent of the parts. It was my assessment that this student was developmentally ready to progress to the next level of mathematical learning, generalization, and representation.

Source: Professional Portfolio of Rosanna Calabrese

Survey of Student Experience

This worksheet requires students to make connections between literature and their own lives. As an educator it allows me to gain insight about a student's life experiences and integrate that information into instruction.

Matthew's Tantrum   Name_____

Remember a time that you were upset like Matthew in the book in the book <u>Matthew's Tantrum</u> by Jan Hill.

Write three adjectives that describe how you felt when you were upset.

_____   _____   _____

Draw a picture of what you looked like when you were upset.

What made you upset?

What did you or someone else do to make you feel better?

How is this the same or different than the way Matthew's tantrum was solved?

Outcome: As a result of this connection between life and literature, the students were very eager to share their experiences. The students articulated their thoughts very clearly and were excited to discuss their tantrums in the small group setting. While it may not be "acceptable" to admit crying to second grade peers, my students were elated to find commonalities among their diverse home experiences.

 These artifacts show how a teacher uses knowledge of the learner to plan instruction. Each of these artifacts provides introductions, explanations, and the outcomes of the activity.

Source: Professional Portfolio of Rosanna Calabrese

K-W-L-S

K (What I Know Now)-W (What I Want to Know)-
L (What I Learned)-S (What I Still Want to Know)

Objective: The K-W-L-S chart strategy allows me to assess student background knowledge, identify misconceptions, develop student-directed inquiry lessons, plan lessons that integrate their interest and questions, as well as document student development and growth.

Description: Prior to initiating an interdisciplinary thematic unit on recycling, I took an inventory of student background knowledge. I asked students to think about their forthcoming field trip to the Recycling Center. I asked "What do you already know about recycling?" Student responses varied from "My family composts!" to "I can make stuff out of trash."

After discussing our experience with recycling, I posed another question to my students. "When we go on the field trip, what will you want to know about recycling?" The students used their personal interests to generate a list of questions. My students used these to focus their inquiry at the Recycling Center.

As a result of this survey of student knowledge and interest, I was able to design a unit that attended to their concerns. I developed activities that meet the needs and interests of the learners within my classroom community.

Source: Professional Portfolio of Rosanna Calabrese

A Stimulating Experience

Objective: I wanted my students to experience the differences between urban, rural, and suburban communities. I did this by changing the classroom layout to simulate the spatial relationships among these three communities.

What happened here?!

Students express surprise ov

Description: The students entered the find the desks rearranged. In one cor side. In the middle of the room eight d four desks were completely removed fr This rearrangement was to demonstr communities.

The students predicted why the r what each area of the room represente observations about the traffic, noise le classroom. The day concluded wi commonalities, their differences, and wl

Source: Professional Portfolio of Rosanna Calabrese

Describing methods you use for experiential learning—such as this simulation activity— demonstrates your creativity in instruction.

Include documents that show how you assess student learning.

Formal Assessment

I designed this formal assessment to elicit a variety of higher order thinking skills, as well as to provide a context for the students to apply their concepts of rural, urban, and suburban communities. I consulted Bloom's Taxonomy of Learning to target the types of thinking skills that would incorporate concrete and abstract thinking. This type of assessment provides me with concrete documentation of the students' ability to use a variety of higher order thinking skills to apply their knowledge. Here are three of the questions from this assessment.

In what type of community do you think the boy in Sun Up lives and why do you think this?

Look at the map and label each community.

Use this Venn diagram to compare and contrast rural and urban communities

Source: Professional Portfolio of Rosanna Calabrese

This entry includes a short description of an overnight camping trip. It emphasizes special activities beyond the classroom. It helps the portfolio reviewer to understand the importance of this event and the meaning it had for the teacher and students.

Learning Happens Outside of the Classroom

The following are documents of the overnight camping trip that I attended with a fifth grade class. This was an incredible experience for me as it added to my perspective of the many students I was working with in the classroom. I gained a lot of insight into the possible problems and benefits that come with a large scale trip that incorporates learning in many aspects. From this trip I learned many ways to extend learning experiences beyond those within the walls of the classroom. I observed students use their strengths and multiple intelligences as they were engaged in physical, social, and problem-solving activities.

To encourage students to interact with all different students, the teachers chose the students' daily activity groups. We then included students in the process of choosing their tent mates.

As a group leader on this trip, I was a silent member of the team. I facilitated a series of cooperative confidence building activities. It was important to me that the students come up with their own positive solutions to each given problem.

Here you see the Jaguars, our group's chosen name, working together through many different activities in which teamwork is a must! Before and after each activity, we processed as a group about how we could improve and use good cooperative group strategies.

I was excited to see some follow through with these strategies in class when we returned from the trip.

Source: Professional Portfolio of Lauren T. Costas

Dienes' Levels of Mathematical Learning

Description: I believe that in order to design lessons that are developmentally appropriate for the learners in my classroom community, it is imperative for me to understand the different stages of knowledge. In the subject area of math, I rely on NCTM standards as well as Dienes' Levels of Mathematical Learning. With this model, students are able to develop the background knowledge necessary to understand the abstract concepts of math. I chose these stages of development to design and develop a second grade unit on fractions.

Formalization

Flip Flap Book
Making fractions from a given whole. Labeling fractions and ordering from least to greatest.

Symbolization

Fraction Concentration
Applying representation knowledge by analyzing picture and symbol fractions to determine equivalency.

Representation

Tops and Bottoms
by Janet Stevens

Genera[...]

Free Play

Observing co[...]
wh[...]

Source: Professional Portfolio of Rosanna Calabrese

This entry on the left provides an explanation of the theoretical basis for mathematics instruction.

This artifact demonstrates how one teacher represented her reading program. She not only included her goals but how she intended to achieve the goals.

Reading

Overarching Goal: I would like to provide to my students with literary experiences that will be internalized as positive self images as learners and readers and have this evident by their thoughts, actions, and personal goals.

Content

Goal: I want my students to be aware of their comprehension of written text. My goal for them is to recognize and appreciate that each piece of writing follows a general text structure that allows the reader to comprehend the purpose, setting, and central message of theme.

Actions
- Read literature across genres to illustrate common text structure
- Provide contents for student to analyze and summarize literature based on story structure
- Identify authors' purpose, audience, topic, and form
- Facilitate and develop student investigative skills and curiosity in order to discover the content of their reading
- Integrate literature across the curriculum

Attitude

Goal: I want my students to develop a genuine appreciate for the power and beauty of thoughts written down. In this sense, I would like my student to have accurate connections about reading, as well as possess positive feelings about interacting in a language rich literary environment.

Actions
- Expose students to a variety of genres that address their interests and experiences
- Demonstrate personal passion and enthusiasm for reading
- Provide students with literature that is authentic, meaningful, developmentally appropriate and offers reasonable challenges
- Incorporate reading and writing activities that allow students to articulate thoughts and regard them as valid and legitimate

Process

Goal: I would like my students to be metacognitively aware of the skills and strategies they possess and need to develop to process written language and information. This involves the students' ability to decode written language and make sense of the text.

Actions
- Expose students to pre, during, and post reading strategies
- Model reading strategies such as the context, semantic, and syntax cues to decode text
- Practice prediction, evaluation, summarization, and other thinking skills to assign meaning to text

Source: Professional Portfolio of Rosanna Calabrese

Source: Professional Portfolio of Scott Mooney

Using Computers as a Mode for Instructional Delivery

The use of technology in the classroom has been gaining momentum for many years. I feel fortunate that I am entering the field at this time due to the fact that I can utilize my expertise with computers to assist my students' gaining as much as possible out of various electronic learning aids. Weekly trips to the computer lab as well as daily use of a computer in the classroom can aid the students in their preparation for life in the "real world." Having students use as many programs as possible, such as the Internet, word processing applications, and even learning HTML, will prove to them that they are capable of the successful use of a sometimes scary medium.

Teachers know that using the Internet in class is a daunting challenge in that the students have the opportunity to work on projects that would not be approved of by the teacher or school administration. I understand the risks involved with using technology in the classroom and advocate the close supervision of students at all times when they are using computers in any capacity. The risk of having one bad apple spoil the bunch is too great to allow for anything less than full cooperation by the students with all appropriate rules and regulations rega...

 Provide information about your repertoire of skills in the use of technology. Here are three ways of representing your competencies and use of technology in the classroom.

Using a Survey to Determine Computer Usage

Students who are required to complete essays or other assignments on a word processing machine tend to receive higher grades. This correlation may result from the ease with which the teacher can read
students are required to type out their as
writing while they type. For most student
lag time allows students to think through

To determine if I can expect my class to b
year I will administer this questionnaire.
much as possible about the students' prev
their daily usage. If a majority of my stu
count on being able to attempt more comp
class of novice computer users. I will also
students are capable of finding access to
assignments. This will be extremely impor
weekend.

Name:

Address:

Phone #:

Mother's Name:

Father's Name:

Do you have a computer in your home?

If not, do you have easy access to a compu

How much have you used a computer in the

How much have you used a computer in the

If you were given an assignment that calle
you be able to find an instrument to fulfill

If no, why not?

Source: Professional Portfolio of Scott Mooney

Internet and Computer Skills

Web Author:
- Created Drew-Freeman Middle School's World Wide Web site
- Responsible for maintaining World Wide Web site
- http://www.radix.net~drewfreeman/

Internet Instructor:
- Introduction to the Internet course for teachers in Prince George's County Public Schools accreditation program

Computer Proficiency:
- Windows 3.1 - 95
- HTML 3.0
- Java
- DOS
- Unix
- Mac
- IBM

Source: Professional Portfolio of Ryan Imbriale

Peer Evaluation

Objective: Peer and self-assessments allow students to develop their evaluative skills. They become responsible for determining the quality of their work. This empowers the students, as well as provides me with a framework to collaboratively evaluate students.

Author's Name: _____ Story _____			
The author identified the characters in the story.	☺	☹	☹
The author told where the story took place.	☺	☹	☹
The author mentioned the story's problem and how it was resolved.	☺	☹	☹
The author told the main idea in the first sentence.	☺	☹	☹
The author stuck to the topic of the paragraph.	☺	☹	☹

 Include unique methods for evaluation such as this peer evaluation example.

Description: One of my reading groups re... recognized that the tale was a reflection of the... author, not an original work. I asked the stude... in the form of a paragraph. We discussed th... paragraph structure and decided what would be... I created this evaluation sheet based on their sug... read their summary paragraphs to each other... with this form and then discussed their react... utilized constructive criticism and the rubric to...

Source: Professional Portfolio of Rosanna Calabrese

Be sure to include documents that provide information about your effectiveness as a teacher. Artifacts can be notes or letters from students, parents, administrators, and supervisors as well as solicited feedback received from a survey such as the one shown here.

How Am I Doing?

Hey, class!!! Remember me? I actually want your opinion about my teaching. Please complete the following evaluation. Be fair in your assessment, but most of all—be honest!!

Please circle the number that rates my performance.

(1: very poor . . . . 5: excellent)

1.	Enthusiasm	1	2	3	4	5
2.	Attitude	1	2	3	4	5
3.	Fairness	1	2	3	4	5
4.	Knowledge	1	2	3	4	5
5.	Creativity	1	2	3	4	5
6.	Interest	1	2	3	4	5

Comments:

Source: Professional Portfolio of Jeff Maher

Friday Folders and Anecdotal Records

One of the routines that my cooperating teacher and I established from the first week of school was the use of Friday Folders. During each week all morning work, class work, and handwriting papers are filed in each student's Friday Folder. The folders are kept in the students' desks and it is their responsibility to keep track of their folder and its contents. On Thursday, my cooperating teacher and I take the folders home to check. While checking, I kept detailed anecdotal records of each student's progress in the units we were studying. The records also kept track of missing and incomplete work. On Friday, the students took their folders home to share their work with their families. On Monday, the folders return to school empty and ready for the next week. The process of keeping anecdotal records of student progress had both given me practice in record keeping, and taught me to give attention to EVERY child's progress EVERY week. I was able to see patterns in missing assignments and note which students did not understand which concepts. This insight gave me the information needed to provide additional assistance to the students based on their individual needs. The following is a sample of my anecdotal records.

Include examples of how you monitor and assess your students' progress.

Source: Professional Portfolio of Emily Anne Cosden

Friday Folder Anecdotal Records 2/24/00

Student A - All papers present and complete. Understands solids and liquids. Can move to schedule portion of time unit.

Student B - Front of Tuesday's math paper incomplete. Continues to confuse the minute and hour hands.

Student C - Keep an eye on her cursive n's. Needs practice describing objects using all of her senses.

Student D - Does not use the lines on the paper for handwriting. Continues to confuse the hour and minute hands.

Student E - Wednesday's morning work incomplete. Progressing with writing more legibly.

Student F - Wednesday's science paper incomplete. Understands solids and liquids.

Student G - Did not follow directions on Tuesday's morning work. Needs to practice describing objects using all of her senses.

Source: Professional Portfolio of Emily Anne Cosden

Bibliography of Special Education Related Topics

Harris, K. R., Graham, S., & Deshler, D. (Eds.). (1998). <u>Teaching every child every day: Learning in diverse schools and classrooms.</u> Cambridge, MA: Brookline Books.

*Hart, E. R., & Speece, D. L. (1998). Reciprocal teaching goes to college: Effects for postsecondary students at risk for academic failure. <u>Journal of Educational Psychology, 90,</u> 670-68.

Lieber, J., Schwartz, I. S., Sandall, S., Horn E., & Wolery, R. A. (1999). Curricular considerations for young children in inclusive settings. In C. Seefeldt (Ed.). <u>Early childhood curriculum: A review of the research</u> (pp. 243-264). New York: Teachers College Press.

Mamlin, N., & Harris, K.R. (1998). Elementary teacher's referral to special education in light of inclusion and prereferral: "Every child is here to learn…but some of these children are in real trouble." <u>Journal of Educational Psychology, 90</u> (3), 385-396.

Sexton, M., Harris, K.R., & Graham, S. (1998). Self-regulated strategy development and the writing process: Effects on essay writing and attributions. <u>Exceptional Children, 64,</u> 3, 295-311.

Speece, D.L., MacDonald V., Kilsheimer L., & Krist, J. (1997). Research to practice: Pr&

> In order to individualize instruction for all students, I have independently researched strategies and theories related to special education. As a regular education classroom teacher, my current interests focus on ways I can help and improve instruction for included students faced with motivation, attention, and learning challenges. The sources listed above are among those resources that I have consulted and studied. I plan to earn a Master's Degree in Special Education.
>
> After student teaching, I was hired as a long-term substitute social studies teacher for the remainder of the school year. I taught two ninth grade inclusion classes and three self-contained special education classes for eighth, tenth, and eleventh grades.

Source: Professional Portfolio of Merritt Imbriale

Transcripts, descriptions of courses or workshops attended, test scores, honors, or awards will validate your academic accomplishments. However, there are other ways to document your ongoing pursuit of knowledge. The above entry includes a short bibliography of articles read with a brief explanation of how this information is intended to be used. It also contains plans for future professional growth.

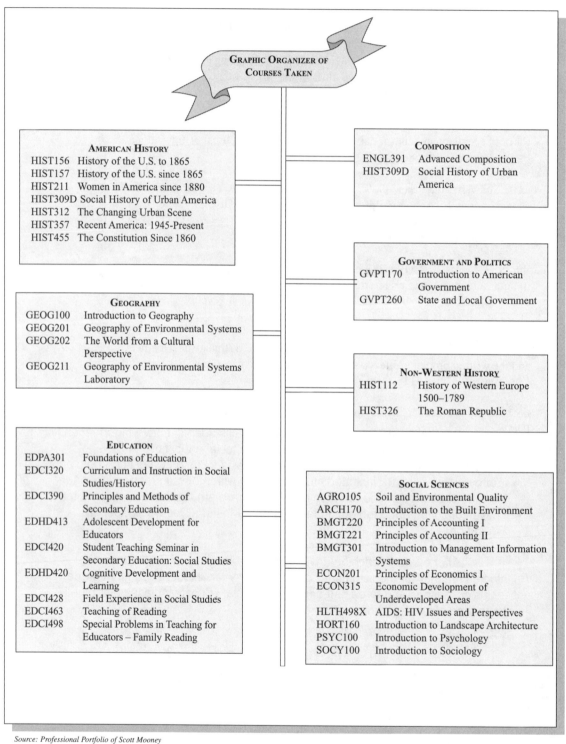

GRAPHIC ORGANIZER OF COURSES TAKEN

AMERICAN HISTORY
HIST156   History of the U.S. to 1865
HIST157   History of the U.S. since 1865
HIST211   Women in America since 1880
HIST309D Social History of Urban America
HIST312   The Changing Urban Scene
HIST357   Recent America: 1945-Present
HIST455   The Constitution Since 1860

COMPOSITION
ENGL391   Advanced Composition
HIST309D   Social History of Urban
           America

GOVERNMENT AND POLITICS
GVPT170   Introduction to American
           Government
GVPT260   State and Local Government

GEOGRAPHY
GEOG100   Introduction to Geography
GEOG201   Geography of Environmental Systems
GEOG202   The World from a Cultural
           Perspective
GEOG211   Geography of Environmental Systems
           Laboratory

NON-WESTERN HISTORY
HIST112   History of Western Europe
           1500–1789
HIST326   The Roman Republic

EDUCATION
EDPA301   Foundations of Education
EDCI320   Curriculum and Instruction in Social
           Studies/History
EDCI390   Principles and Methods of
           Secondary Education
EDHD413   Adolescent Development for
           Educators
EDCI420   Student Teaching Seminar in
           Secondary Education: Social Studies
EDHD420   Cognitive Development and
           Learning
EDCI428   Field Experience in Social Studies
EDCI463   Teaching of Reading
EDCI498   Special Problems in Teaching for
           Educators – Family Reading

SOCIAL SCIENCES
AGRO105   Soil and Environmental Quality
ARCH170   Introduction to the Built Environment
BMGT220   Principles of Accounting I
BMGT221   Principles of Accounting II
BMGT301   Introduction to Management Information
           Systems
ECON201   Principles of Economics I
ECON315   Economic Development of
           Underdeveloped Areas
HLTH498X   AIDS: HIV Issues and Perspectives
HORT160   Introduction to Landscape Architecture
PSYC100   Introduction to Psychology
SOCY100   Introduction to Sociology

Source: Professional Portfolio of Scott Mooney

This graphic organizer is a creative way to highlight the courses most relevant to your area of certification. It can be an impressive supplement to your transcript.

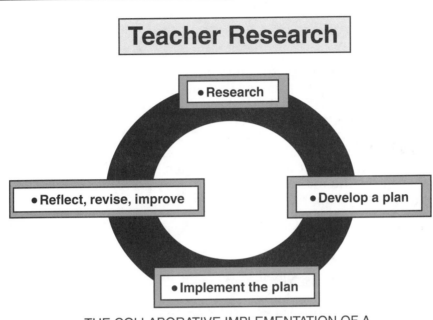

THE COLLABORATIVE IMPLEMENTATION OF A
WRITING WORKSHOP IN A SECOND GRADE CLASSROOM

Abstract

This teacher research project revolved around the following research questions: How do we begin a writers' workshop in this second grade classroom? How do we continually improve it? What insights can we gain about children and the writing process? The process encompassed the collaboration of my cooperating teacher, myself, and the students in a suburban to rural area of southern Maryland. These students were a heterogeneous group of diverse backgrounds, including 21% African American, 12% Hispanic, and 67% Caucasian. The literature review gives an overview of the three schools of thought regarding writing: the cognitive information processing theories, the Piagetian/naturalist theories, and the social-constructionist theories. Methodology included background research on writing workshops, observation of a writing workshop in a fourth grade classroom, and reflective collaborations with my cooperating teacher as well as with the students. Methods of data collection included interviewing 46% of the students, a questionnaire for my cooperating teacher and me, homework assignments for all students, the students' writing workshop folders that documented their writing process, and the students' finished books. In analyzing the data, I used the technique of triangulation, which involves the gathering of information from three different points of view: my cooperating teacher's, my students', and my own. The internal validity is strengthened through the manner in which the multiple methods of data collection complement and check each other. The findings included a high percentage (73% of those interviewed) speaking of writing as something that helps them to learn. The majority (82% of those interviewed) cited that the act of writing itself helped them to become better writers. The study revealed that creative freedom motivated most of the students, that a special education student could be included in a meaningful manner, and that second graders can see themselves as authors.

Source: Professional Portfolio of Carol Dungan

This portfolio entry shows how one teacher conducted research to improve classroom instruction and increase student learning.

Source: Professional Portfolio of Denise Logsdon

Videotape Introduction

A video was made of an introductory lesson on patterning. The students had previously done work with patterning two objects, but this was their first opportunity to pattern three different objects.

This video first includes an example of guided practice on patterning being done by the teacher. Then viewers can see the individual students as they are engaged in making patterns of three objects.
of instr

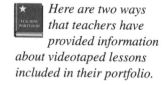

Here are two ways that teachers have provided information about videotaped lessons included in their portfolio.

My Journey in Pictures: Video Critique
(Approx. 1 hour)

Clip #1: Who's in the Shed?
Strategies Seen in This Clip:

-The flashlight in this lesson was used as a motivational tool for this lesson. Notice how focused the children are during the reading and how the flashlight enables them to easily follow along.

-As I read the story, several times I asked students to share their predictions. Not only did this give students practice in using this skill, but it also kept them involved with the story and allowed them to share their individual ideas with the whole group.

-A management strategy that I used with the children during this lesson was allowing them to pat their heads when they had the same prediction as another student. This prevented other children from calling out "Yeah, I was going to say that." In addition, the strategy also encouraged students to really listen to each other's ideas as they spoke.

-A final strategy that I used was a reminder to students to "think in their head" and not call out/raise their hands. I used this because I wanted each child to have enough wait time to think of his or her own prediction without the influence of others.

Clip #2: Big Hungry Bear
Strategies Seen in This Clip:

-Interactive chalkboard writing: Students used inventive spelling by sounding out words and writing them on their own individual chalkboards. This technique kept all students involved throughout the lesson. The chalkboards also allowed me to informally assess student participation and abilities.

-I used the "stop and listen" technique to gain students' attention before giving directions.

Source: Professional Portfolio of Kate Maczis

Reflection

Reflecting on my knowledge of the learner brings me back to each individual child whom I have worked with. Especially those certain few, who drained me of all of energy, challenged my assumptions, and caused me to grow. There is always a child who gives you feedback, such as the letters seen in this section, that reminds you of your purpose as an educator. The responsibility of encouraging individual differences, expanding minds and potentials, is part of that purpose.

How do you handle the student nobody likes? How about the student who stays up all night playing Nintendo? What about the students who get all of the support in the world, and then those who get none? It is a challenging dilemma, and one a teacher faces every day because inevitably all of these factors affect a child's school perfo[...] cannot be ignored.

Students have different needs. As [...] and more about each student, I learn mo[...] about how to become a better teacher [...] those differences in my classroom. I fe[...] that my compassion for children an[...] development will always motivate me [...] meet children at their individual levels.

Source: Professional Portfolio of Lauren T. Costas

These examples of reflective entries represent teachers' thoughts, feelings, and insights about their teaching experience.

REFLECTIONS ON TEACHING

Many students have trouble acknowledging that they need help in art. Perhaps this is because what they produce is clearly visible to their peers. Understanding the nature and fragility of the young ego, I try and scout for students showing signs of confusion or trouble. Instead of putting them on the spot and embarrassing them, I make suggestions and try to help them to solve the problems for themselves. I have noticed that this can allow the student to take full credit for having overcome an obstacle and adds to his or her positive self-concept.

Source: Professional Portfolio of Mat DeMunbrun

News from Mrs. D's 4th Grade Class
January, 2001

Special Events:
The students from Mrs. D's 4th grade class will be participating in the following events:

- Art Show: February 5
- Field trip to Museum: March 20
- Science Fair: April 10
- School Play: May 9
- Physical Fitness Day: June 8

Keep your eyes open for flyers that explain the details of each of these special events.

Reminders:
- PTA meeting for February 10 will be at 7:00 p.m. in the multi-purpose room.
- Please remember to bring your canned food donation. Our class is in second place for the school-wide drive.

Start saving your used books for our March 22nd book sale. Mark your calendar NOW!

Three Cheers for the Readers of the Week!!!!

Congratulations to:
Cindy L.
Maleka E.
Greg G.
Michael F.
Takita M.
Tyrone P.

These students have read 10 or more books in the past month.

Classroom Highlights:

- We will begin our new science unit on preserving the environment next week.
- We are progressing rapidly in our higher level understanding of the use of fractions and decimals.
- The election was the best possible experience we could h...
  m...
  u...
- o...
  b...

These two examples relate to developing productive relationships with parents. This entry is a newsletter that keeps parents informed about classroom events.

Dealing with a Difficult Parent

One of the most significant learning experiences that I had during my student teaching involved interacting with a very difficult parent. The first week of school this parent began expressing displeasure with her son's education. She articulated disapproval of everything from his reading materials to the presence of a student teacher in his classroom. These and other concerns continued to present themselves throughout the year. From this experience I learned many strategies for handling this type of parent without placing any additional stress on anyone. During the second week of school, we began a communication log between my cooperating teacher, myself, and the parent. This log was taken home every night and returned the next day. In the log, the parent was able to express any of her concerns about her son or his education. We were able to easily address all of her concerns without taking away from class or planning time to speak on the phone. Another advantage of the communication log was that there was a record of every concern and all of our attempts to address the concerns. We also kept precise records of all telephone conversations. We were able to refer back to the communication log and the telephone records during conferences with the parent. Our extensive attention and detailed records gave the parent the feeling that she was being listened to and her concerns were considered valid. Gradually, the parent grew to trust us and, consequently, her concerns lessened. We were able to give this parent the attention and validation that she needed without putting her or ourselves in an uncomfortable position.

Source: Professional Portfolio of Emily T. Cosden

The entry above describes a strategy that was implemented to work more effectively with a parent.

REFLECTION
. . . is a KEY to professional and personal growth.

What Is the Relationship Between Teaching and Learning?

For me, teaching and learning are inseparable. I believe that for true teaching to take place, learning must accompany it. And for learning to take place, teaching must be present in some form. Learning is to be valued more than teaching, for it is the reason teaching exists. This topic is a deep and involved one that cannot possibly be covered in this essay, but I will comment on some thoughts I have begun to form in this area.

First of all, I would like to say that I now understand that there is much more involved in learning to teach than I initially anticipated. I realize now that there is no recipe for being the perfect teacher. It is an art and a skill that will be continually built upon all of my life. One of the greatest gifts that this program has given to me is the opportunity to be reflective. This has encouraged me to "stimulate and facilitate significant and self-reliant learning" (Rogers, 1969). I cannot think of anything more important in my beginning and refining as a teacher than that of taking charge of my own learning process. It will be a worthy lifelong endeavor.

If somehow my own love for learning could be passed on to my students, it would begin to make a difference in their lives. I am in agreement with Suzanne Wilson (1990) when . . .

Source: Professional Portfolio of Carol Dungan

In order for the reviewer to have a more in-depth perspective of you as a reflective practitioner and problem solver, it is important to include your thoughts, feelings, and learnings that provide insight about your growth as a professional teacher. Keep in mind that reflections can be integrated throughout the entire portfolio in context with the artifact or can be used as an introduction or conclusion to a portfolio section.

Appendix A:
Examples of Standards

Interstate New Teacher Assessment and Support Consortium (INTASC) Standards

The ten statements presented here are the basic principles underlying the knowledge, dispositions, and performances deemed essential for all BEGINNING TEACHERS, regardless of their specialty areas. They are specifically intended to address behaviors that constitute what novice teachers need to practice responsibly when they enter the teaching profession. A complete copy of the standards, including knowledge, dispositions, and performances, can be obtained by contacting the Council of Chief State School Officers, One Massachusetts Avenue NW, Suite 700, Washington, DC 20001-1431.

Principle 1: The teacher understands the central concepts, tools of inquiry, and structures of the discipline(s) he or she teaches and can create learning experiences that make these aspects of subject matter meaningful for students.

Principle 2: The teacher understands how children learn and develop and can provide learning opportunities that support their intellectual, social, and personal development.

Principle 3: The teacher understands how students differ in their approaches to learning and creates instructional opportunities that are adapted to diverse learners.

Principle 4: The teacher understands and uses a variety of instructional strategies to encourage students' development of critical thinking, problem solving, and performance skills.

Principle 5: The teacher uses an understanding of individual and group motivation and behavior to create a learning environment that encourages positive social interaction, active engagement in learning, and self-motivation.

Principle 6: The teacher uses knowledge of effective verbal, nonverbal, and media communication techniques to foster active inquiry, collaboration, and supportive interaction in the classroom.

Principle 7: The teacher plans instruction based upon knowledge of subject matter, students, the community, and curriculum goals.

Principle 8: The teacher understands and uses formal and informal assessment strategies to evaluate and ensure the continuous intellectual, social, and physical development of the learner.

Principle 9: The teacher is a reflective practitioner who continually evaluates the effects of his or her choices and actions on others (students, parents, and other professionals in the learning community) and who actively seeks out opportunities to grow professionally.

Principle 10: The teacher fosters relationships with school colleagues, parents, and agencies in the larger community to support students' learning and well-being.

Source: Interstate New Teacher Assessment and Support Consortium (INTASC), Council of Chief State School Officer (CSSO).

NBPTS Early Childhood/Generalist Standards

Three- to Eight-Year-Olds

The requirements for certification as an Early Childhood/Generalist are organized around the following eight standards. These standards have been ordered as portant facets of the art and science of teaching young children. In fact, in the course of excellent early childhood teaching, teachers often demonstrate several of these standards concurrently as they skillfully weave their knowledge, skills, and dispositions into a rich tapestry of exemplary practice.

I. *Understanding Young Children*
Teachers use their knowledge of child development and their relationships with children and families to understand children as individuals and to plan in response to their unique needs and potentials.

II. *Promoting Child Development and Learning*
Teachers promote children's physical, emotional, linguistic, creative, intellectual, social, and cognitive development by organizing the environment in ways that best facilitate the development and learning of young children.

III. *Knowledge of Integrated Curriculum*
On the basis of their knowledge of academic subjects and how young children learn, teachers design and implement developmentally appropriate learning experiences within and across the disciplines.

IV. *Multiple Teaching Strategies for Meaningful Learning*
Teachers use a variety of methods and materials to promote individual development, meaningful learning, and social cooperation.

V. *Assessment*
Teachers know the strengths and weaknesses of various assessment methodologies, continually monitor children's activities and behavior, and analyze this information to improve their work with children and parents.

VI. *Reflective Practice*
Teachers regularly analyze, evaluate and strengthen the quality and effectiveness of their work.

VII. *Family Partnerships*
Teachers work with and through parents and families to support children's learning and development.

VIII. *Professional Partnerships*
Teachers work with colleagues to improve programs and practices for young children and their families.

Source: Reprinted with permission from the National Board for Professional Teaching Standards, Early Childhood Standards, 1998, all rights reserved.

Performance Standards: The Council for Exceptional Children

Special education professional standards are governed foremost by the CEC Code of Ethics and a common core of knowledge and skills. The information below represents the skills section from the document entitled *What Every Special Educator Must Know: International Standards for the Preparation and Certification of Special Education Teachers*. For a complete set of standards contact The Council for Exceptional Children, 11110 North Glebe Road, Suite 300, Arlington, VA 22201-5704.

1. Philosophical, Historical, and Legal Foundations of Special Education
   - Articulate personal philosophy of special education including its relationship to/with regular education.
   - Conduct instructional and other professional activities consistent with the requirements of law, rules and regulations, and local district policies and procedures.
2. Characteristics of Learners
   - Access information on various cognitive, communication, physical, cultural, social, and emotional conditions of individuals with exceptional learning needs.
3. Assessment, Diagnosis, and Evaluation
   - Collaborate with families and other professionals involved in the assessment of individuals with exceptional learning needs.
   - Create and maintain records.
   - Gather background information regarding academic, medical, and family history.
   - Use various types of assessment procedures appropriately.
   - Interpret information from formal and informal assessment instruments and procedures.
   - Report assessment results to individuals with exceptional learning needs, parents, administrators, and other professionals using appropriate communication skills.
   - Use performance data and information from teachers, other professionals, individuals with exceptionalities, and parents to make or suggest appropriate modification in learning environments.
   - Develop individualized assessment strategies for instruction.
   - Use assessment information in making instructional decisions and planning individual programs that result in appropriate placement and intervention for all individuals with exceptional learning needs, including those from culturally and/or linguistically diverse backgrounds.
   - Evaluate the results of instruction.
   - Evaluate supports needed for integration into various program placements.

4. Instructional Content and Practice
   - Interpret and use assessment data for instructional planning.
   - Develop and/or select instructional content, materials, resources, and strategies that respond to cultural, linguistic, and gender differences.
   - Develop comprehensive, longitudinal individualized programs.
   - Choose and use appropriate technologies to accomplish instructional objectives and to integrate them appropriately into the instructional process.
   - Prepare appropriate lesson plans.
   - Involve the individual and family in setting instructional goals and charting progress.
   - Conduct and use task analysis.
   - Select, adapt, and use instructional strategies and materials according to characteristics of the learner.
   - Sequence, implement, and evaluate individual learning objectives.
   - Integrate effective, social, and career/vocational skills with academic curricula.
   - Use strategies for facilitating maintenance and generalization of skills across learning environments.
   - Use instructional time properly.
   - Teach individuals with exceptional learning needs to use thinking, problem solving, and other cognitive strategies to meet their individual needs.
   - Choose and implement instructional techniques and strategies that promote successful transitions for individuals with exceptional learning needs.
   - Establish and maintain rapport with learners.
   - Use verbal and nonverbal communication techniques.
   - Conduct self-evaluation of instruction.

5. Planning and Managing the Teaching and Learning Environment
   - Create a safe, positive, and supportive learning environment in which diversities are valued.
   - Use strategies and techniques for facilitating the functional integration of individuals with exceptional learning needs in various settings.
   - Prepare and organize materials to implement daily lesson plans.
   - Incorporate evaluation, planning, and management procedures that match learner needs with the instructional environment.
   - Design a learning environment that encourages active participation by learners in a variety of individual and group learning activities.
   - Design, structure, and manage daily routines, effectively including transition time, for students, other staff, and the instructional setting.
   - Direct the activities of a classroom paraprofessional, aide, volunteer, or peer tutor.

- Create an environment that encourages self-advocacy and increased independence.

6. Managing Student Behavior and Social Interaction Skills
   - Demonstrate a variety of effective behavior management techniques appropriate to the needs of individuals with exceptional learning needs.
   - Implement the least intensive intervention consistent with the needs of the individuals with exceptionalities.
   - Modify the learning environment (schedule and physical arrangement) to manage inappropriate behaviors.
   - Identify realistic expectations for personal and social behavior in various settings.
   - Integrate social skills into the curriculum.
   - Use effective teaching procedures in social skills instruction.
   - Demonstrate procedures to increase the individual's self-awareness, self-control, self-reliance, and self-esteem.
   - Prepare individuals with exceptional learning needs to exhibit self-enhancing behavior in response to societal attitudes and actions.

7. Communication and Collaborative Partnerships
   - Use collaborative strategies in working with individuals with exceptional learning needs, parents, and school and community personnel in various learning environments.
   - Communicate and consult with individuals, parents, teachers, and other school and community personnel.
   - Foster respectful and beneficial relationships between families and professionals.
   - Encourage and assist families to become active participants in the educational team.
   - Plan and conduct collaborative conferences with families or primary caregivers.
   - Collaborate with regular classroom teachers and other school and community personnel in integrating individuals with exceptional learning needs into various learning environments.
   - Communicate with regular teachers, administrators, and other school personnel about the characteristics and needs of individuals with specific exceptional learning needs.

8. Professionalism and Ethical Practices
   - Demonstrate commitment to developing the highest educational and quality-of-life potential of individuals with exceptional learning needs.
   - Demonstrate positive regard for the culture, religion, gender, and sexual orientation of individual students.
   - Promote and maintain a high level of competence and integrity in the practice of the profession.

- Exercise objective professional judgment in the practice of the profession.
- Demonstrate proficiency in oral and written communication.
- Engage in professional activities that may benefit individuals with exceptional learning needs, their families, and/or colleagues.
- Comply with local, state, provincial, and federal monitoring and evaluation requirements.
- Use copyrighted educational materials in an ethical manner.
- Practice within the CEC Code of Ethics and other standards and policies of the profession.

Source: Copyright 1997–2000 by The Council for Exceptional Children. Reprinted by permission.

Appendix B:
Professional Organizations

American Alliance for Health, Physical Education, Recreation and Dance
1900 Association Drive
Reston, VA 20191
(800) 213-7193; (703) 476-3400
www.AAHPERD.org

American Council on the Teaching of Foreign Languages
6 Executive Plaza
Yonkers, NY 10701
(914) 963-8830
www.actfl.org

American Library Association
50 E. Huron Street
Chicago, IL 60611
(800) 545-2433
www.ala.org

Association for Childhood Education International
17904 Georgia Avenue, Suite 215
Olney, MD 20832
(800) 423-3563; (301) 570-2111
www.acei.org

Council for Exceptional Children
1110 North Glebe Road, Suite 300
Arlington, VA 22201-5704
(888) 232-7733; (703) 264-9446
www.cec.sped.org

Council of Chief State School Officers
One Massachusetts Avenue NW, Suite 700
Washington, DC 20001-1431
(201) 408-5505
www.ccsso.org/intasc.html

National Association for Music Education
1806 Robert Fulton Drive
Reston, VA 20191
(800) 336-3768; (730) 860-4000
www.menc.org

National Art Education Association
1916 Association Drive
Reston, VA 20191-1590
(800) 299-8321; (703) 860-8000
www.naea-reston.org

National Association of Biology Teachers
   12030 Sunrise Valley Drive
   Suite 110 Reston, VA 20191
   (800) 406-0775; (703) 262-9696
   www.NABT.org

National Association for the Education of Young Children
   1509 16th Street NW
   Washington, DC 20036-14266
   (202) 232-8777; (800) 424-2460
   www.NAEYC.org

National Board for Professional Teaching Standards
   26555 Evergreen Road, Suite 400
   Southfield, MI 48076
   (800) 229-9074; (248) 351-4444
   www.NBPTS.org

National Council for the Social Studies
   3501 Newark Street NW
   Washington, DC 20016
   (202) 966-7840
   www.NCSS.org

National Council of Teachers of English
   1111 Kenyon Road
   Urbana, IL 61801
   (800) 369-6283
   www.NCTE.org

National Council of Teachers of Mathematics
   1906 Association Drive
   Reston, VA 20191-9988
   (800) 235-7566; (703) 620-9840
   www.NCTM.org

National Science Teachers Association
   1840 Wilson Boulevard
   Arlington, VA 22201-3000
   (800) 722-6782; (703) 243-7100
   www.NSTA.org

Appendix C:
Worksheet: Linking Coursework Standards to Portfolio Documents

Directions:
- Identify the course.
- List the assignments.
- Determine how the assignment contributed to your knowledge, disposition, and skills.
- Identify the performance standard this supports.
- Reflect in writing what you learned.
- Consider what could be placed in your portfolio to capture this experience.

Course	Assignment	Knowledge	Dispositions	Skill	Standard(s)

Reflection:

Possible Portfolio Documents:

Course	Assignment	Knowledge	Dispositions	Skills	Standard(s)

Reflection:

Possible Portfolio Documents:

Appendix D:
Sample Permission Letter for Photographs and/or Videotapes

Date _____

Dear Parent/Guardian,

I am a teacher candidate from (identify your university or teacher training program). Throughout the next (provide time span) weeks, I will be taking pictures and/or videos of a variety of classroom activities to represent teaching experiences during my internship. As part of my teacher education program requirements, I am expected to develop a professional teaching portfolio. I would like to be able to include these pictures and/or videos of classroom activities in my portfolio and I would appreciate your permission to use items that may have your child in them.

These pictures and/or videos are for the purpose of "bringing to life" the documents I present in my professional portfolio. They would remain my personal property and would only be used for educational purposes associated with my teacher education program and for sharing my portfolio during employment interviews.

Please check one of the two statements below, sign, and return this document

to _____

_____ I grant permission for my child to be photographed and/or videotaped in an instructional setting for educational purposes and for the photographs to be included in the teacher candidate's professional portfolio.

_____ I do not give permission for my child to be photographed and/or videotaped for any reason.

Student's Name _____

School _____

Teacher's name _____

Signature of
parent/guardian _____

Date _____

Sincerely,

Teacher Candidate

cc: Principal

Appendix E:
Including a Videotape
in Your Portfolio

Some teachers choose to provide a videotape of their teaching as part of their portfolio documentation. This is an excellent idea; however, you will need to include some type of introduction of your video that will increase the viewer's understanding of the lesson. Remember to keep the video short, between ten and twenty minutes. Be sure that the video shows a balance of your teaching and student involvement. You can include an introduction to the lesson at the beginning of the videotape and your analysis of the lesson at the end.

Videotape Information

Teacher's Name _____   Grade Level _____

Subject Area   _____

Description of setting and class/group:

Title of Lesson _____ Viewing Time _____

Lesson Objective and Rationale:

Description of the teaching episode (background information related to the lesson or portion of instruction taped):

Suggested focus areas when viewing the tape:

Results of instruction and/or evidence of learning:

Personal reflections and analysis of teaching:

Appendix F:
Worksheet: Making Decisions About Potential Portfolio Documents

This worksheet is intended to help you think about what you already have and what you need to begin the collection of documents for your portfolio. Keep in mind that the documentation you include should be your own materials, designed and developed by you, and not copies of commercially developed products.

Documents and validation materials I currently have that support the purposes of my portfolio.	*Materials I need to create or obtain to enhance this area (including introductions, explanations, and reflections.*	*Which performance standard or theme does this support?*

Educational philosophy

Planning for instruction

Instructional units I have developed and taught

	Documents and validation materials I currently have that support the purposes of my portfolio.	*Materials I need to create or obtain to enhance this area (including introductions, explanations, and reflections.*	*Which performance standard or theme does this support?*
 *My repertoire of instructional strategies*			
 *Technological skills*			
 *Evidence of a multicultural perspective*			

	Documents and validation materials I currently have that support the purposes of my portfolio.	*Materials I need to create or obtain to enhance this area (including introductions, explanations, and reflections.*	*Which performance standard or theme does this support?*
 *Evidence of how I have included all students in my instruction*			
 *Classroom management/discipline*			
 *Parent, teacher, student conferences*			

Documents and validation materials I currently have that support the purposes of my portfolio.	*Materials I need to create or obtain to enhance this area (including introductions, explanations, and reflections.*	*Which performance standard or theme does this support?*

Subject matter competency

Diagnosis and assessment of student learning

Professional development activities

	Documents and validation materials I currently have that support the purposes of my portfolio.	Materials I need to create or obtain to enhance this area (including introductions, explanations, and reflections.	Which performance standard or theme does this support?
 *Community involvement*			
 *Travel, hobbies, talents, skills, and other experiences that influence my teaching and enhance the educational program*			
 *Professionalism*			
 *Letters, notes, recommendations, and evaluations*			

Appendix G:
Worksheet: Self-Evaluation

Instructions: After considering the questions posed in each section, answer with a **yes** or **no**, then rate yourself with an *E = excellent, S = satisfactory, NI = needs improvement.* If you have rated any section of your portfolio with an *S* or *NI*, think about what you could do to give yourself a rating of excellent. Write your ideas for improving the quality of your portfolio in the action plan section. When you believe that you have represented yourself the best that you can, you are ready to present your portfolio.

	Introduction and Organization of Portfolio	*Performance Standards, Themes, or Goals*
Definition	The introduction sets the stage for the content of your portfolio. It is the opening statement that includes information regarding your philosophy of teaching, learning, or leadership and may include your professional goals that relate to the purpose of your portfolio. Portfolio organization refers to the way the portfolio is assembled.	Performance standards identify the knowledge, dispositions, and skills that a teacher should know and be able to demonstrate. They provide the conceptual framework for portfolio development and documentation. *Goals* identify areas for professional development. They correlate with performance standards or themes. *Themes* are generic categories that are inherent throughout the performance standards.
Attributes That Promote Quality Portfolios	____ Is my introduction meaningful, informative, and related to the purpose of my portfolio? ____ Does my introduction include a strong rationale for inclusion of the selected documents? ____ Did I include my philosophy of education? ____ Are the contents housed logically? ____ Are artifacts organized effectively? ____ Are the artifacts easily accessible? ____ Did I include a plan for continued professional development?	____ Are performance based standards, themes, or goals used as the foundation for my portfolio documentation? ____ Is there evidence in my portfolio that communicates how I have used standards, goals, or themes? ____ Did I include a cross reference chart?
Action Plan for Polishing and Refining My Portfolio		

Documentation	Introductions, Explanations, and Reflections
Documentation refers to the artifacts selected to support your professional competencies. They may be a combination of teacher-made materials, student work, evaluation documents completed by others that validate your professional performance, and additional materials as appropriate to the purpose of the portfolio.	These are narrative entries that provide information about the documents and insight about the portfolio developer's thoughts related to teaching and learning.
____ Are all my artifacts relevant to the purpose? ____ Are my artifacts directly related to a standard(s), theme(s), or goal(s)? ____ Do the artifacts provide substantial evidence in support of my competency and growth toward that standard(s), theme(s), or goal(s)? ____ Do I have a variety of artifacts organized thoughtfully and displayed effectively? ____ Are my artifacts accompanied by introductions, explanations, and reflections? ____ Are my evaluative documents current and completed by professionals who have first hand knowledge of my performance? ____ Do my artifacts show significant evidence to support student learning and/or the results of my instruction?	____ Are my introductions at the beginning of each section clearly articulated? Do they provide a rationale for inclusion of the forthcoming documents, linkage to my philosophical beliefs, and comments about how the documents support the standard, theme or goal? ____ Do my explanations clearly describe the document and its relevance to the standard, goal, theme, or purpose of my portfolio? ____ Do my explanations provide other information to help the reviewer understand how this entry supports my ability to teach, impact student learning, or demonstrate leadership? ____ Do my reflections provide evidence of my ability to think critically, problem solve, make decisions, relate theory to practice, learn from experience, and/or grow professionally?

Appendix H:
Overall Portfolio Assessment Instrument

Directions: Place an X on the continuum that reflects your evaluation of each of the following portfolio aspects. Use the Comments section to provide feedback regarding your assessment.

1. Introduction to Portfolio

1	2	3	4	5

Provides little or no information about the purpose, organization, and rationale for selection of documents

Provides significant information about the purpose, organization, and rationale for the selection of documents

Comments:

2. Philosophy Statement

1	2	3	4	5

Lacks personalization and not educationally sound

Personalized and educationally sound

Comments:

3. Standards, Themes, Goals

1	2	3	4	5

No obvious evidence that performance standards, themes, or goals have been considered

Clearly evident that performance standards, themes, or goals have been considered

Comments:

4. Documentation

1	2	3	4	5

Limited artifacts that lack substance, have little meaning, and do not provide adequate evidence in support of performance standards, themes, or goals

Variety of artifacts that have significant substance and meaning and provide irrefutable evidence in support of performance standards, themes, or goals

Comments:

5. Introductions and Explanations Accompanying Artifacts

1	2	3	4	5

Narratives lack clarity and do not provide enough information related to the artifacts and their relevance to the performance standards, themes, or goals

Clearly articulated narratives that provide substantial information related to the artifacts and their relevance to the performance standards, themes, or goals.

Comments:

6. Reflective Entries

1	2	3	4	5
Narratives unclear, lacking insight, critical thinking, and problem solving, and show no evidence of commitment to growth and learning				Narratives are very clear, reveal significant insight, critical thinking, problem solving, and serious commitment to growth and learning

Comments:

7. Professional Development Plan

1	2	3	4	5
Plan is not appropriate to the professional needs of the individual and does not identify goals for a higher level of performance				Plan is most appropriate in meeting the professional needs of the individual and identifies goals for a significantly higher level of performance

Comments:

8. Writing Mechanics

1	2	3	4	5
Narratives unclear, with many errors in grammar, spelling, and punctuation				Narratives clearly articulated, with no errors in grammar, spelling, or punctuation

Comments:

9. Organization and Appearance of Portfolio

1	2	3	4	5
Messy, unprofessional appearance, unorganized, and difficult to locate documents				Neat, professional appearance, logical organization, and easy access to documents

Comments:

10. Overall Rating

1	2	3	4	5
Unsatisfactory portfolio that does not support teaching competencies		Satisfactory portfolio that adequately supports teaching competencies		Outstanding portfolio that irrefutably supports teaching competencies

Comments:

Overall Comments and Recommendations:

Appendix I:
Example Portfolio Contents

Villa Julie College, Stevenson, Maryland

Portfolio preparation is seen as a process and takes place over the course of three years of preservice teaching experience. Although the nature of portfolios is that each student's work is unique, there are certain characteristics common to most portfolios at each stage. The following contents are required for the exit portfolio, graduation, and completion of the student teaching internship.

Contents for Exit Portfolio

Credentials

- Resume
- References
- Transcripts
- NTE scores
- GPA
- Final evaluations from supervising teachers and college supervisor

Professional Development

- Professional development plans
- Short- and long-term teaching goals
- Self-assessment of goals set and goals achieved
- Specific data about the schools assigned: name of schools, addresses, phone numbers, names of supervising teacher(s), principal, and university supervisor
- List of pertinent activities, responsibilities, and observations regarding the above named schools
- Summary of professional growth workshops given or attended
- Evaluation/reflection of other professional development efforts
- Professional organizations and responsibilities
- Honors and awards

Source: This material is reprinted by permission of Dr. Deborah Kraft, Villa Julie College.

Philosophy and Reflection

- Reflective responses that provide the insight into the student's knowledge, skills, philosophy, or professional perceptions as a teacher
- Personal logs or weekly self-assessments from field placements

Teaching Strategies and Methodology/Planning, Implementation, and Evaluation of Instruction

- Samples of written lesson plans
- Methods and strategies used to integrate
  — multicultural perspectives
  — inclusion
  — learning disabilities
  — varying learning styles and modalities
  — classroom management and behavioral problems
  — application of technology
- Samples of assignments and projects developed for children
- Products/samples of students' (children's) work
- Written evaluations from the supervising teacher, college supervisor, peer coach, and others
- Interdisciplinary unit
- Photos of any special activities or projects including captions
- Samples of bulletin boards (include photos if available)
- Videotape of teaching a lesson with attached critiques

Communication and Human Relations Skills

- Samples of parental communications
- Parental involvement
- Peer coaching experiences
- Clippings and articles about field placement class, school, or self from school newsletter and local paper
- Letters of appreciation and commendation

Personal Skills

- Volunteerism
- Special talents and skills

Source: This material is reprinted by permission of Dr. Deborah Kraft, Villa Julie College.

EDUCATION DEPARTMENT

SCORING RUBRIC FOR THE EXIT PORTFOLIO

A composite score of 3 or above for each Dimension of the rubric and each General Trait is required. Students who receive any score of 1 or 2 will be given an opportunity to revise and resubmit their portfolio

Points	DIMENSIONS OF TEACHING			GENERAL TRAITS		
	Written Documentation	Reflections	Visuals	Language	Organization	Presentment
	This trait refers to written content that includes lesson plans, narratives, course assignments, and tables used to document knowledge & skills in Dimension.	*This trait refers to expressed thoughts or opinions resulting from careful consideration of evidence used to document knowledge & skills in Dimension.*	*This trait refers to pictures, graphics, charts, or videos used to demonstrate knowledge & skills in Dimension.*	*This trait refers to the use of the conventions of standard written English, such as grammar, mechanics, word usage, and spelling.*	*This trait refers to the manner in which the contents of the portfolio are arranged to demonstrate student's unique skills and abilities.*	*This trait refers to the overall appearance of the portfolio and the manner in which the appearance of the portfolio orients the reader.*
5 Exceptional	•Demonstrates: -Critical thought & reasoning -Breadth and depth of understanding •Provides substantial description & explanation	•Demonstrates: -Critical thought & reasoning -Breadth and depth of understanding •Provides substantial description & explanation	•Extensive and outstanding use of visuals to demonstrate knowledge & skills in Dimension •Visuals of consistently high quality greatly enhance demonstration of knowledge & skills in Dimension	•Outstanding use of the conventions of standard written English.	•Follows a focused and logical organization •Clearly shows original thinking •Highly imaginative	•Professional quality •Impresses the reader •Outstandingly clear, bright, and colorful
4 Thorough	•Demonstrates: -Careful thought & reasoning -Clear understanding •Provides fair description	•Demonstrates: -Careful thought & reasoning -Clear understanding •Provides fair description	•Excellent use of visuals to demonstrate knowledge & skills in Dimension •Visuals enhance demonstration of knowledge & skills in Dimension	•Effective use of the conventions of standard written English	•Follows a logical organization •Demonstrates careful thought •Distinctive	•Distinctive appearance •Effectively orients reader •Consistently clear, bright, colorful
3 Adequate	•Demonstrates: -Superficial thought & reasoning -General understanding •Provides fair descriptions	•Demonstrates: -Superficial thought & reasoning -General understanding •Provides fair descriptions	•Sufficient use of visuals to demonstrate knowledge & skills in Dimension •Visuals used •Average quality	•Minor errors in the use of the conventions of standard written English	•Fair organization •Demonstrates thought	•Acceptable appearance •Reader's orientation is generally maintained •Generally clear, bright, colorful
2 Inadequate	•Demonstrates: -Limited thought & reasoning -Incomplete understanding •Provides vague descriptions	•Demonstrates: -Limited thought & reasoning -Incomplete understanding •Provides vague descriptions	•Minimal use of visuals to demonstrate knowledge & skills in Dimension •Quality of visuals varies	•Several errors in the use of the conventions of standard written English	•Organization is confusing or hard to follow	•Inconsistent appearance •Confusing orientation for the reader •Inappropriate use of color
1 Unacceptable	•No evidence of: -Thought & reasoning -Understanding •No description or explanation	•No evidence of: -Thought & reasoning -Understanding •No description or explanation	•No visuals to demonstrate knowledge & skills in Dimension	•Extensive errors in the use of the conventions of standard written English	•No apparent organization	•Poor, sloppy appearance •Does not orient reader

This material is reprinted by permission of Dr. Deborah Kraft, Villa Julie College.

VILLA JULIE COLLEGE * STEVENSON, MARYLAND 21153-0614

EDUCATION DEPARTMENT

SCORING FOR THE EXIT PORTFOLIO

A composite score of 3 or above for each Dimension of the rubric and each General Trait is required. Students who receive any score of 1 or 2 will be given an opportunity to revise and resubmit their portfolio

Student: Date:

Assessed by:

Dimension	SCORE			
	Written Documentation	Reflections	Visuals	Composite Score
1. Demonstrate mastery of appropriate academic disciplines and teaching techniques.				
2. Demonstrate an understanding that knowledge of the learners' physical, cognitive, emotional, and socio-cultural development as the basis for effective teaching.				
3. Incorporate a multicultural perspective which integrates culturally diverse resources, including those from the learner's family and community.				
4. Demonstrate a knowledge of strategies for integrating students with special needs into the regular classroom.				
5. Use valid assessment approaches, both formal and informal, which are age appropriate and address a variety of developmental needs, conceptual abilities, curriculum outcomes, and school goals.				
6. Organize and manage a classroom using approaches supported by research, best practice, expert opinion, and student learning needs.				
7. Use computer and computer-related technology to meet student and professional needs.				
8. Demonstrate an understanding that classrooms and schools are sites of ethical, social, and civic activity.				
9. Collaborate with the broad educational community including parents, businesses, and social service agencies.				
10. Engage in careful analysis, problem-solving and reflection in all aspects of teaching.				

General Trait*	Score
Language	
Organization	
Presentment	

Additional required content: *(refer to page 33 of the Education Handbook)*

Resume
Credentials
Evaluations
Professional Development Plan

This material is reprinted by permission of Dr. Deborah Kraft, Villa Julie College.

135

George Mason University, Graduate School of Education

The Professional Development Portfolio: A Performance-Based Document

Introduction

The Professional Development Portfolio is a requirement for the successful completion of a licensure program but is only one of several factors considered in determining a preservice teacher's readiness for teaching. The product is designed around university program goals and published professional standards that represent the professional consensus of what beginning teachers should know and be able to do. The Interstate New Teacher Assessment and Support Consortium (INTASC) articulated the ten standards incorporated into this document. The evaluation of the portfolio and its presentation will be integrated with the overall evaluation of the program work and internship. The Professional Development Portfolio may also be used during a job search.

Guidelines for Professional Development Portfolio

The following recommendations will be helpful to preservice teachers preparing the portfolio:

- The portfolio is an evolving document and should be continually in a state of development.
- The portfolio should be comprised of pieces that the intern has selected because they are significant examples of growth. Faculty and teachers may suggest entries.
- The appearance of the portfolio should not overshadow its contents; however, an organized document demonstrates careful thought and preparation.
- Each section of the portfolio should include a reflective statement in which the intern examines the samples included and analyzes their significance.
- Reflections should not merely provide a description of the material included, but should tell why a particular item or strategy was chosen, what the student learned through an experience or what he or she would do differently/similarly the next time, and how the student might use this information in the future to improve his or her professional practice.

Portfolio Contents and Format

The Professional Development Portfolio, as an evolving, formative document, should be organized in a looseleaf binder to allow for good organization, easy access to materials, and frequent updating. The eight required sections provide the framework for the portfolio. Below are suggestions of sample products that could be included under each. All of these suggestions need not be included. Choose the piece of evidence that best illustrates each section. **Each section should contain a reflective statement**.

Source: This material is reprinted by permission of Rebecca K. Fox, George Mason University, Graduate School of Education.

Title Page

Table of Contents

I.   **Professional Documentation**
      Résumé
      Philosophy of Education—provides information about the intern's educational beliefs and evolving philosophy of education. The essay should address the preservice teacher's perceptions of him- or herself as a developing teacher and state the individual's philosophy of education.

II.   **Content Pedagogy and Planning (INTASC Standards 1 and 7)**
      Provides information and evidence about actual classroom instruction, lesson preparation, and class time management.
      Possible Items for Inclusion:
      Instructional unit and lesson plans—select examples of most growth or best work, with examples of work done by students (with appropriate permission) and planned forms of assessment for Unit/Daily Lesson Plans
      Instructional materials developed by the intern
      Evidence of adaptations or accommodation to these lesson plans for various learning styles, abilities, instructional levels, interests, and needs of students taught
      Photographs of classroom activities

III. **Student Development and Learning (INTASC Standards 2, 3, and 4)**
      Provides evidence that the teacher can evaluate student performance to design instruction appropriate for social, cognitive, and emotional development.
      Possible Items for Inclusion:
      Example(s) of instructional design appropriate to students' stages of development, learning styles, strengths, and needs (i.e., an example of a lesson resulting from an assessment)
      Evidence of multiple teaching and learning strategies used to meet the needs of diverse learners (i.e., example of a single lesson using numerous teaching strategies)
      Evidence of teacher knowledge of appropriate services or resources available/used to meet exceptional learning needs of students when needed (i.e., an interview with a reading specialist or resource teacher)

IV.   **Motivation and Classroom Management (INTASC Standard 5)**
      Captures how the teacher creates a rich classroom environment that is supportive of working in his or her setting with learners who have varied learning styles and needs.
      Possible Items for Inclusion:
      List of successful strategies used in the classroom
      Description or diagram of classroom with explanation
      Photographs of bulletin boards and learning environment

V.   **Communication and Technology (INTASC Standard 6)**
      Shows how the preservice teacher models effective communication strategies in conveying ideas and information and uses a variety of media communication tools to enrich learning opportunities.

Source: This material is reprinted by permission of Rebecca K. Fox, George Mason University, Graduate School of Education.

Possible Items for Inclusion:

Examples of different types of technology used in the classroom (i.e., WebQuests, lists of websites used, software programs, videos) to enrich learning opportunities

Student products—with appropriate permission

Compilation of websites used for professional research or class preparation

Example of a lesson plan that incorporates technology

VI.   Assessment Strategies (INTASC Standard 8)

Possible Items for Inclusion:

Compilation of assessment techniques used for authentic and performance-based assessment

Case study of an individual, with summary of assessment strategies

Evidence of assessment strategies you have used in the classroom (i.e., student examples, rubrics created and used)

VII.   Reflective Practice: Professional Development (INTASC Standard 9)

Provides evidence that the teacher uses classroom observation, information about students, and research as sources for evaluating the outcomes of teaching and learning; uses professional literature, colleagues, and other resources to support self-development as a learner and as a teacher.

Possible Items for Inclusion:

Reflective statement (includes a portion that will be completed at the conclusion of the student teaching internship to respond to the following questions: How have your educational philosophy and goals changed as a result of your student teaching experience? What types of professional development do you now see as important? What are your goals as a professional educator?)

Documentation from the student teaching internship, which might include:

Observation reports completed by the university supervisor or mentor teacher

Bi-weekly progress reports

Evidence of the development of reflective practice—Journal entries or excerpts from a teaching journal, reflections of a lesson

Videotape and self-observation report of a lesson taught

VIII.   School and Community Involvement (INTASC Standard 10)

Provides information about and evidence of communication/collaboration with parents and/or other professionals within the school and with parents/guardians.

Possible Items for Inclusion:

Evidence of communication with parents/guardians, school community, students and/or colleagues (letters to or other communication with parents/guardians and students, solicitation of their help in classroom or on other projects)

Evidence of attendance at and involvement in team or departmental meetings (i.e., notes taken)

Evidence of participation in collegial activities designed to promote a productive learning environment in the school community

Source: This material is reprinted by permission of Rebecca K. Fox, George Mason University, Graduate School of Education.

Portfolio Evaluation

Student _____ Date _____

University Supervisor_____

Evaluation by:

_____ University Supervisor _____ Student (Self) _____ Cooperating Teacher

Directions: Please evaluate each of the areas below using the following rating scale:

5 = Excellent,   4 = Good,   3 = Satisfactory,   2 = Marginal,   1 = Unsatisfactory

_____ Philosophy of Education: Contains personal statement of philosophy of education; reflects evolution in beliefs about teaching/learning process; includes statement of professional goals

_____ Résumé: Quality of copy; acceptable format; relevant professional experiences included

_____ Content Pedagogy and Planning: Documentation entries demonstrate growth and careful choice. Integration evident through choices of unit and daily goals and objectives; planning includes assessment measures; examples include work done by the students and instructional materials developed by the intern; evidence provided for adaptations or accommodation for various learning styles and needs; plans reflect the intern's philosophy of education

_____ Student Development and Learning: Provides example(s) of instructional design appropriate to students' stages of development, learning styles, strengths, and needs. Provides evidence of multiple teaching and learning strategies used to meet the needs of diverse learners (i.e., example of a single lesson using numerous teaching strategies included).

_____ Motivation and Classroom Management: Presents an example of an environment supportive of working with learners of many styles and needs; careful thought evident; procedures carefully thought through. Includes successful strategies used in the classroom by intern and evidence of classroom management style. Strategies support intern's philosophy of education statement.

_____ Communication and Technology: Provides examples/evidence of use of technology in the classroom and evidence of student learning outcomes.

_____ Assessment Strategies: Provides several examples of assessment strategies and techniques used in the classroom; strategies support the intern's philosophy of education statement.

_____ Reflective Practice—Professional Development: Demonstrates careful thought and reflection as a teacher practitioner who evaluates his or her choices and actions; provides evidence of intern's ability to work toward goal of continuous reflective teaching; provides evidence of intern's awareness of strengths and growth during the student teaching internship. Shows support of intern's philosophy of education statement.

_____ Family and Community Involvement: Information provided about communication

Source: This material is reprinted by permission of Rebecca K. Fox, George Mason University, Graduate School of Education.

and/or collaboration with parents or guardians and/or other professionals in the school and surrounding community; includes evidence of communication with parents/families to support students' learning and well-being.

_____ Overall Organization and Appearance of Portfolio

_____ Presentation by Intern

_____ OVERALL EVALUATION OF THE PROFESSIONAL DEVELOPMENT PORTFOLIO

ADDITIONAL COMMENTS:

Source: This material is reprinted by permission of Rebecca K. Fox, George Mason University, Graduate School of Education.

Glossary

Artifacts, documents, entries, and materials: Terms used interchangeably referring to the contents of the portfolio.

Dispositions: The attitudes teachers develop to think and act in a manner that is professionally acceptable.

Electronic portfolio (digital or computer-generated portfolio):   The electronic portfolio, sometimes referred to as a digital portfolio or a computer-generated portfolio, is a multimedia approach that is typically published on the World Wide Web (WWW) or CD-ROM. The electronic portfolio allows the teacher to present teaching, learning, and reflective artifacts in a variety of media formats (audio, video, graphics, and text).

Entrance portfolio: A collection of specific materials required by a teacher education program as a component of the screening and admissions process.

Exit portfolio: A final selection of specific artifacts that provide substantial evidence of a teacher candidate's knowledge, dispositions, and skills of teaching and/or fulfilling the requirements of the teacher education program. This portfolio may be required to successfully complete the teacher education or certification program.

Explanations: Narratives that provide information about the artifact presented. They provide a better understanding of the document that cannot be captured by the artifact alone.

HTML: A format that tells a computer how to display a Web page. The documents themselves are plain text files (ASCII) with special *tags* or codes that a Web browser knows how to interpret and display on a computer screen.

Hypermedia: Units of information that are interconnected by links.

Hypermedia "card" program: A software program that allows the integration of graphics, sound, and movies in a single file. Electronic cards or screens are linked together by developer-created buttons.

Inservice teacher: An individual who is employed by the school or school system as a classroom teacher or specialist.

INTASC standards: A set of teaching performances that includes the knowledge, dispositions, and skills expected of the beginning teacher. The standards were established by the Interstate New Teacher Assessment and Support Consortium (INTASC).

Interview portfolio: A polished selection of exemplary documents and reflective entries that represent a teacher candidate's best work and accomplishments.

Introductions: Narratives that are usually found at the beginning of the portfolio or at the onset of each new section with the intent to provide an overview of the forthcoming material.

Knowledge: A foundation of information about teaching, learning, and students that provides the basis for informed decision making.

Multimedia: The presentation of information in more than one format, e.g., video, audio, graphics, or text.

Multimedia slideshow software: Software that allows the portfolio developer to create electronic slides that incorporate sound and video in a linear sequence.

NBPTS standards: A set of high and rigorous performances standards that identify what accomplished teachers should know and be able to do. These standards were established by the National Board for Professional Teaching Standards (NBPTS).

PDF documents: A universal file format that preserves all of the fonts, formatting, colors, and graphics of any source document, regardless of the application and platform used to create it.

Performance standards: Shared views within the education community of what constitutes professional teaching. Standards include the knowledge, dispositions, and skills of the effective teacher.

Phases of portfolio development: A step-by-step method for working through the entire portfolio development process.

Preservice teacher: Individuals who are enrolled in a teacher education program or teacher certification program; also referred to as teacher candidates, student teachers, or teaching interns.

Professional development plan: A teacher's set of activities that are based on identified goals for professional growth.

Professional teaching portfolio: A selection of artifacts and reflective entries representing a teacher's professional experiences, teaching competencies, and growth over a period of time.

Reflection: A process that requires careful and analytical thinking about issues related to the teaching profession; a highly complex thinking process that is cultivated over time.

Showcase portfolio: A polished collection of exemplary documents and reflective entries that highlight an inservice teacher's best work and accomplishments.

Skills: The ability to transfer knowledge of teaching and learning into behaviors necessary for effective teaching.

Web-authoring software: Software programs that will translate text and graphics into an HTML format.

Working portfolio (inservice):   A collection of teaching artifacts and reflections that provide ongoing evidence of a teacher's growth and accomplishments related to his or her goals for ongoing professional development.

Working portfolio (preservice):   A collection of teaching artifacts and reflections that provide ongoing evidence of a teacher candidate's growth at various benchmarks throughout the teacher education program.

References

146   REFERENCES

Ambach, G. (1996, November). Standards for teachers, potential for improving practice. *Phi Delta Kappan, 78,* 207–210.

Anderson, R. S., & DeMuelle, L. (1998, Winter). Portfolio use in twenty-four teacher education programs. *Teacher Education Quarterly, 25,* 23–31.

Antonek, J. L., McCormick, D. E., & Donato, R. (1997, Spring). The student teacher portfolio as autobiography: Developing a professional identity. *The Modern Language Journal, 81,* 5–27.

Aschermann, J. R. (1999) Electronic portfolios: Why? What? How? In SITE 99: *Society for Information Technology & Teacher Education International Conference* (ERIC Reproduction Service No. ED 432 305).

Barrett, H. C. (1999). Electronic teaching portfolios. In SITE 99: *Society for Information Technology & Teacher Education International Conference* (ERIC Reproduction Service No. ED 432 265).

Barrett, H. C. (2000). Create your own electronic portfolio: Using off-the-shelf software to showcase your own or student work. *Learning and Leading with Technology, 27* (7), 14–21.

Barry, N. H., & Shannon, D. M. (1997). Portfolios in teacher education: A matter of perspective. *The Educational Forum, 61* (4), 320–328.

Bartell, C. A. (1998). A normative vision of teacher as professional. *Teacher Education Quarterly, 25* (4), 24–30.

Bartell, C. A., Kaye, C., & Morin J. A. (1998). Portfolio conversation: A mentored journey. *Teacher Education Quarterly, 25* (1), 129–39.

Barton, J., & Collins, A. (1993). Portfolios in teacher education. *Journal of Teacher Education, 44* (3), 200–210.

Bernauer, J. A. (1999). Emerging standards: Empowerment with purpose. *Kappa Delta Pi Record, 35* (2), 68–70.

Bird, T. (1990). The schoolteacher's portfolio: An essay on possibilities. In J. Millman & L. Darling-Hammond, (Eds)., *The new handbook of teacher evaluation: Assessing elementary and secondary school teachers* (2nd ed.; pp. 241–256). Newbury Park, CA: Sage.

Boulware, Z. M., & Holt, D. M. (1998). Using CD-ROM technology with preservice teachers to develop portfolios. *T.H.E. Journal, 26* (2), 60–62.

Brown, J. D., & Wolfe-Quintero, K. (1997). Teacher portfolios for evaluation: A great idea? Or a waste of time? *The Language Teacher, 21* (1), 28–30.

Cushman, K. (1999). Educators making portfolios. *Phi Delta Kappan, 80* (6), 744–750.

Darling-Hammond, L. (1997). *What matters most: Teaching for America's future.* Washington, DC: The National Commission of Teaching and America's Future.

Darling-Hammond, L., Wise, A., & Klein, S (1995). *A license to teach: Building a profession for 21st century schools.* Boulder, CO: Westview Press.

Draper, W. (1998). Turning challenge into opportunity. *Kappa Delta Pi Record, 34* (3), 155.

Evans, S. M. (1995). *Professional portfolios: Documenting and presenting performance excellence.* Virginia Beach, VA: Teacher's Little Secrets.

Georgi, D., & Crowe, J. (1998). Digital portfolios: a confluence of portfolio assessment and technology. *Teacher Education Quarterly, 25,* 73–84.

Goldsby, D. S., & Fazal, M. B. (2000). Technologies answer to portfolios for teachers. *Kappa Delta Pi Record, 36* (3), 121–123.

Guillaume, A. M., & Yopp, H. K. (1995). Professional portfolios for student teachers. *Teacher Education Quarterly, 22* (1) 93–101.

Hunter, A. (1998). The power, production, and promise of portfolios for novice and seasoned teachers. In *Portfolio models: Reflections across the teaching process.* Norwood MA: Christopher-Gordon Publishers.

Interstate New Teacher Support and Assessment Consortium. (1992). *Model standards for beginning teacher licensing and development: A resource for state dialogue.* Washington DC: Council of Chief State School Officers.

Jackson, D. (1997). Developing student generated computer portfolios. *Teaching and Teacher Education Annual, 2,* 698–700.

McKinney, M. O. (1998). Preservice teachers' electronic portfolios: Integrating technology, self-assessment, and reflection. *Teacher Education Quarterly, 25,* 85–103.

Milman, N. (1999). Web-based electronic teaching portfolios for preservice teachers. In SITE 99: *Society for Information Technology & Teacher Education International Conference* (ERIC Reproduction Service No. ED 432 273).

National Commission on Teaching and America's Future. (1996, September). *What matters most: Teaching for America's future.* New York: Author.

Rakow, S. J. (1999). Involving classroom teachers in the assessment of preservice intern portfolios. *Action in Teacher Education, 21* (1), 108–15.

Riggsby, D., Jewell, V., & Justice, A. (1995). Electronic portfolio: Assessment, resume, or marketing tool? In *Association of Small Computer Users in Education (ASCUE) Summer Conference Proceedings* (ERIC Reproduction Service No. ED. 387-115).

Stone, B. A. (1998, Winter). Problems, pitfalls and benefits of portfolios. *Teacher Education Quarterly, 25,*105–114.

Wheeler, P. H. (1993). *Using portfolios to assess teacher performance* (EREAPA Publication Series No. 93-97). Livermore, CA: EREAPA Associates.

Wiedmer, T. L. (1998). Digital portfolios: Capturing and demonstrating skills and levels of performance. *Phi Delta Kappan, 79* (8), 586–89.

Wolfe, K. (1991). The schoolteacher's portfolio: Issues in design, implementation, and evaluation. *Phi Delta Kappan, 73* (2), 129–136.

Wolfe, K., & Dietz, M. E. (1998) Teaching portfolios: Purposes and possibilities. *Teacher Education Quarterly, 25* (1), 9–22.

Index

A

Ambach, G., 10
Anderson, R.S, 5
Antonek, J.L., 3
Artifacts
    instructional, examples of, 71–97
    introductory, examples of, 58–71
Aschermann, J.R., 48, 51
Assessment instrument, overall portfolio, 127–129
Assessment strategies, 36

B

Barrett, H.C., 47, 48, 50, 51
Barry, N.H., 3
Bartell, C.A., 4, 9
Barton, J., 4, 6
Bernauer, J.A., 9
Bird, T., 2
Boulware, Z.M., 48
Brown, J.D., 2

C

CD burners, 51
CD portfolios, 48
Classroom management and organization, 26
Collaboration, promoting, 5
Collins, A., 4, 6
Common language, 11
Council for Exceptional Children (CEC), 11
Council of Chief State School Officers, 100
Credibility, 10
Crowe, J., 54
Current artifacts, 24
Cushman, K., 5

D

Darling-Hammond, L., 10
DeMuelle, L., 5
Dietz, M.E., 4
Dispositions, 142
Documents
    displaying, 32–36
    formatting, 35
    housing, 33–35
    organizing, 35
    presentation of, 6–7
Donato, R., 3
Draper, W., 11

E

Electronic portfolio, 47–55
    additional information, locating, 52–53
    computer hardware, 49
    computer software, 50
    defining, 47–48
    helpful hints, 53–54

publishing options and issues, 51
    CD, 51
    Internet, 51–52
reasons for developing, 48
technological skills, 49
Enhancing documents, 29–39
    connecting standards to portfolio documentation, 29–30
    displaying, 32–36
        formatting, 35
        housing, 33–35
        organizing, 33–35
    portfolio entry, teaching experience as, 36–39
    support for documents, 30–32
        explanations, 31
        introductions, 31
        reflections, 31–32
Entrance portfolio, 3, 41
ERIC database, 52
Essential Dimensions of Teaching, 17
    figure, 20
Evans, S.M., 2
Exit portfolio, 3, 41
    scoring rubric for, Villa Julie example, 134–135
Explanations, 31

F

Fazal, M.B., 47, 48
Formatting, 35

G

Georgi, D., 54
Goldsby, D.S., 47, 48
Guillaume, A.M., 3

H

Holistic approach to assessment, providing, 6
Holt, D.M., 48
Housing, 33
Human relationships, 26
Hunter, A., 6
Hypermedia, 142
Hypermedia links, 48

I

Inservice teacher portfolio, 4
    showcase portfolio, 4
    working portfolio, 4
Instruction, delivery and assessment of, 24
Instructional artifacts, examples of, 71–97
    assessing learning in mathematics, 83
    assessing student learning, 85
    assessments and results of student learning, 72
    bibliography of articles read, 91
    courses relevant to area of certification, 92
    daily lesson plan, 76

demonstrated reading program, 87
developing productive relationships with
     parents, 96
experiential learning, 85
facilitated thinking and problem solving, 81
feedback from survey, 89
graphic organizer, 72
home, school, community experiences, 79
implementing various behavior management
     strategies, 75
improving classroom instruction, research, 93
interdisciplinary approach, 71
introductions and reflections, 71
introductory lesson, social studies unit, 82
journal writing, 83
managing and organizing the classroom, 73, 74
monitoring and assessing students' progress, 90
multicultural perspective in the classroom, 77, 78
peer evaluation, 89
photographed example of an activity, 72
providing insight on growth as a professional
     teacher, 97
scoring rubric, 81
simulation activity, 85
special activities beyond the classroom, 86
students' contribution to a group activity, 82
theoretical basis for mathematics instruction, 87
thoughts, feelings, and insights on teaching, 95
unit outline, 72
use of technology in the classroom, 88
using learner's knowledge to plan instruction,
     84
videotaped lessons, 94
weekly plan, 76
working more effectively with a parent, 96
INTASC standards, 142
Internet-based portfolio, 48
Interstate New Teacher Assessment and Support
     Consortium (INTASC), 9
     standards, 100
Interview portfolio, 3, 41
Introductions, explanations, and reflections
     combined, figure, 34
Introductory artifacts, examples of, 58–71
     electronic portfolio home page, 60
     knowledge of subject matter, 68
     narratives, 62
     performance in the area of pedagogy, 70
     performance standards, cross-reference of, 65
     performance standards and portfolio
          documentation, 64
     philosophy of education, 63
     planning and instructional delivery, 69
     professional goals, 66, 67
     table of contents, 58–59
     teacher's philosophy of education, 63

J
Jackson, D., 47, 48, 54
Jewell, V., 48
Justice, A., 48

K
Kaye, C., 4
Klein, S., 10

L
Likert scale, 43

M
McCormick, D.E., 3
McKinney, M.O., 47
Milman, N., 48
Morin, J.A., 4
Multimedia slideshow software, 50

N
National Board for Professional Teaching Standards
     (NBPTS), 9
     early childhood/generalist standards, 101
     standards, definition of, 142
National Commission on Teaching, 10
     and America's Future, 9
National School Reform Faculty (NSRF), 5
NTE, 25

O
Organizing, 35

P
Parent-teacher conference experience, portfolio
     entry for, figure, 37
     artifacts related to, figure, 38
PDF documents, 142
PDF formats, 50
Performance standards
     Council for Exceptional Children, 102–105
     and coursework, 12–13
     and professional development plan, 13
Permission letter for photographs and/or
     videotapes, sample, 113–114
Planning, 24
Portfolio, using, 41–46
     presenting, 44–46
     self-evaluating, 41–42
          documentation, 42–43
          introduction and organization of, 42
          introductions, explanations, and reflections, 43
          performance standards, use of, 42
Portfolio contents, examples of, 131–133
Portfolio development
     and performance standards, 9–21
          background, 9–10

Portfolio development, *(cont.)*
  linking standards to teaching and portfolio
      development, 10–21
  process, starting, 23–28
    choosing performance standards, 23–24
    collecting, selecting, and creating documents,
      24
    determining purpose, 23
Portfolio documents/entries
  on CD, 48
  electronic, 47
  evaluation of, 5
  examples of, 57–97
    instructional artifacts, 71–97
    introductory artifacts, 58–71
  linking coursework to standards and, figure, 14
PRAXIS, 25
Preservice teacher portfolio, 3
  entrance, 3
  exit, 3
  interview, 3
  working, 3
Process portfolio, 3
Product portfolio, 3
Professional development plan, process for
      creating, figure, 15–17
Professional development portfolio
  George Mason University, example, 136–140
Professional goals chart, figure, 19
Professionalism, 27
Professional knowledge, 10
Professional organizations, 108–109
Professional teaching portfolio, 1–8
  benefits of portfolio development, 4–6
    fostering self-assessment and reflection, 4
    promoting collaboration, 5–6
    providing holistic approach to assessment, 6
    providing personal satisfaction and renewal, 5
    providing tools for empowerment, 5
  definitions of, 2
  development issues, 6–7
    evaluation of documents, 7
    labor-intensive and time-consuming
        preparation, 6
    presentation of documents, 6–7
  types of
    inservice teacher portfolio, 4
    preservice teacher portfolio, 3

Publishing a portfolio
  on CD, 51
  on the Internet, 51

R
Rakow, S.J., 3
Reflections, 31–32
Riggsby, D., 48

S
Self-assessment and reflection, fostering, 4
Self-evaluation worksheet, 123–126
Seven-step approach as portfolio entry, figure, 18
Shannon, D.M., 3
Showcase portfolio, 4, 41
Standards and artifacts, cross-reference chart, 30
Stone, B.A., 6
Subject matter, knowledge of, 24

T
Targeted outcomes, 10
Teaching dispositions, 10
Teaching skills, 10
Tools for empowerment, providing, 5

V
Videotape, as portfolio element, 115–116

W
Web authoring software, 50
Wheeler, P.H., 6
Wiedmer, T.L., 48
Wise, A., 10
Wolfe, K., 4
Wolfe-Quintero, K., 2
Working portfolio, 3, 4, 41
Worksheets
  linking coursework standards to portfolio
      documents, 111–112
  making decisions about potential portfolio
      documents, 117–122

Y
Yopp, H.K., 3